T0314602

First published by Lawrence Erlbaum Associates, Inc.
10 Industrial Avenue, Mahwah, New Jersey 07430

This edition published 2011 by Routledge

Routledge, Taylor & Francis Group, 711 Third Avenue, New York, NY 10017
Routledge, Taylor & Francis Group, 27 Church Road, Hove East Sussex BN3 2FA

Production Editor: Erica A. Teilborg, *Lawrence Erlbaum Associates, Inc.*

Subscriber Information: *Applied Developmental Science* is published four times a year. Subscriptions for the 2002 volume are available on a calendar-year basis. In the United States and Canada, per-volume rates are US $45 for individuals and US $260 for institutions; in other countries, per-volume rates are US $75 for individuals and US $290 for institutions. Send subscription orders, information requests, and address changes to the Journal Subscription Department, Lawrence Erlbaum Associates, Inc., 10 Industrial Avenue, Mahwah, NJ 07430–2262. Address changes should include the mailing label or a facsimile. Claims for missing issues cannot be honored beyond 4 months after mailing date. Duplicate copies cannot be sent to replace issues not delivered due to failure to notify publisher of change of address.

Electronic: Full-price print subscribers to Volume 6, 2002 are entitled to receive the electronic version free of charge. *Electronic-only* subscriptions are also available at a reduced price of $234.00 for institutions and $40.50 for individuals.

Applied Developmental Science is abstracted or indexed in *Child Development Abstracts & Bibliography; Linguistics and Language Behavior Abstracts; PsycINFO/Psychological Abstracts, Social Planning/Policy & Development Abstracts;* and *Sociological Abstracts.* Microform copies of this journal are available through Bell & Howell Information and Learning, P. O. Box 1346, Ann Arbor, MI 48106–1346. For more information, call 1–800–521–0600 x2888.

APPLIED DEVELOPMENTAL SCIENCE
Volume 6, Number 2

2002

SPECIAL ISSUE:

SCHOOL MATTERS: PATHWAYS TO ACADEMIC SUCCESS AMONG AFRICAN AMERICAN AND LATINO ADOLESCENTS

ARTICLES

Applied Developmental Science
2002, Vol. 6, No. 2, 60–61

School Matters: Pathways to Academic Success Amongst African American and Latino Adolescents

James L. Rodríguez
San Diego State University

Lisa R. Jackson
Boston, Massachusetts

This special issue presents theoretical and empirical studies that provide an understanding of the dynamic, complex, and often conflicting school, family, and community contexts in which African American and Latino adolescents are, formally and informally educated. Focusing on the examination of identity development, family–community background and resources, and academic performance, this special issue is concerned with the development and implementation of culturally relevant policies and programs for African American and Latino adolescents. Two broad questions are addressed in the issue: (1) "What does schooling and academic success mean to African American and Latino adolescents?" and (2) "What impact do school, family, and community contexts have on the academic development and success of African American and Latino adolescents?"

The article by Cooper, Cooper, Azmitia, Chavira, and Guallatt, "Bridging Multiple Worlds: How African American and Latino Youth in Academic Outreach Programs Navigate Math Pathways to College," presents a longitudinal study that uses a challenge model (highlights the interplay of challenges and resources) to examine the college-prep math pathways of African American and Latino adolescents. The authors argue that while universities have offered many outreach programs in an attempt to diversify their campus population, these programs have rarely been studied from a developmental perspective as to what factors foster successful pathways to college. Using the Students' Multiple Worlds Model (Phelan, Davidson, & Yu, 1996), Cooper et al. explains that adolescents are constantly negotiating between the challenges and resources that exist in their families and communities as a way to forge their developmental and academic pathways. Using this perspective, Cooper et al. state predict that, "…youth who coordinate resources and challenges in family, peer, school, and outreach program worlds would achieve higher graders and college eligibility" (p. 74).

The students in the study progressed along one of five pathways that emerged from survey data, academic data sources (e.g., Grade Point Average [GPA], Scholastic Aptitude Test [SAT]), and college choice data. The authors categorized these pathways as steadily high, slowly declining, rapidly declining, increasing, and "back on track" toward college. The authors found that resources and challenges were the strongest predictors of GPA and admission to a prestigious university. Demographic characteristics were not significant predictors of these outcomes. The authors conclude that while it continues to be difficult to generalize findings from studies on outreach programs due to issues such as self-selection and selection criteria, it is, "…through outreach programs, school-based partnerships, and school-to-work programs in the U. S. and other democracies, youth can become part of larger networks of community resources" (p. 86). These community resources can then enhance the network of pathways that African American and Latino students can utilize for academic success.

Constance Yowell examines the role of possible selves in the pursuit of education for Latino youth who continue to have disproportionately high dropout rates. Yowell points out that in trying to understand the cause of dropping out of school, researchers and policy makers often assume that, "students expectations for school success and their academic achievement are significantly related" (p. 62). Yowell argues that in fact the relationship between these two factors is not well understood. She questions whether Latino youth struggle to reconcile the difference between what they dream and hope to become with the reality of limited social mobility in the United States. Drawing on the theory of positive selves by Markus and Nurius (1986), Yowell hypothesizes that,

> …Latino students' expected selves would include more specific procedural knowledge related to goal attainment than either hoped-for or feared selves. It was further hypothesized that in light of this specificity, expected selves would be more likely to predict students' risk status for school dropout than would either hoped-for or feared selves. (p. 62)

Using surveys and student interviews, Yowell worked with ninth grade students in a midwestern high school. What she found was that feared selves, the selves

Requests for reprints should be sent to James L. Rodríguez, College of Education, San Diego State University, 5500 Campanile Drive, San Diego, CA 92182–1153. E-mail: jlrodrig@mail.sdsu.edu that students feared becoming were the strongest predictors of academic performance and risk for dropping out. "Students' fears were embedded in strong visual imagery and affect, an understanding of how their fears may be actualized, and a recognition of the consequences of such actualization" (p. 70). In light of this finding, Yowell offers recommendations aimed at enhancing the educational success of Latino youth specifically in the areas of guidance counseling, school curricula, and dropout prevention. According to Yowell, the key to programs for Latino youth is to provide a meaningful connection between the present contexts in which they live and their expectations for the future.

In a related fashion, Rodriguez' contribution to this issues focuses on the role of family environment in the academic achievement of Mexican American youth. Looking across three generations of Mexican Americans, Rodriguez examined four family environment variables: family involvement, family monitoring, family control, and familism. As an exploratory study, Rodriguez sought to determine the relationship between these variables and academic achievement and how this relationship might vary across generation status.

Using the questionnaire responses of 3,681 high school students, Rodriguez found that third-generation students reported greater family involvement but lower grades than first- or second-generation students. In addition, first and second-generation students reported higher levels of family monitoring than third generation students. Regression analyses revealed a significant relationship between family involvement and monitoring for all three generations of adolescents. Rodriguez concludes that researchers must continue to carefully examine the structure and dynamics of Mexican descent families in order to better understand the family's role in the education and sociocultural development of Mexican descent youth. Furthermore, Rodriguez suggests that researchers, policy-makers, and educators should rethink the appropriateness of applying monolithic and possibly culturally insensitive educational and parent involvement programs to a highly heterogeneous group that is continuously undergoing sociocultural transformation.

Finally, the article by Youngblood and Spencer brings our attention to the experiences of African Americans with special needs in an intervention program. "Specifically, the program is designed to enhance the expression of resiliency (generally as manifested health and mastery demonstrated under conditions of chronic risk) in disabled youth transitioning from school to the world of work and independent living (Spencer, 1999)" (p. 6). The authors demonstrated the importance of such a program to be "culturally sensitive" and "contextually unique" to provide the most effective intervention services to disabled African American youth.

Using interviews and focus group data, the authors describe the experiences of these students as through the lens of an identity-focused cultural ecological perspective. This perspective, "…reinforces the importance of simultaneously considering: (1) the spcieal risk factors, (2) the net effects of supports versus experiences stressors, (3) the reactive coping strategies employed, and (4) the emergent identities manifested" (p. 96). The student interviews provided are examined within this perspective and common themes regarding program design and implementation are discussed.

We hope this special issue provides readers with some theoretical and practical insights of the academic experiences and needs of African American and Latino adolescents. This issue emphasizes the importance of the dynamics of culture and context in understanding the school experiences of these youth in order to develop culturally appropriate policies and programs that effectively support their academic success. Each article in this special issue addresses a set of challenging questions and in the process new questions are raised. The articles in this special issue challenge researchers, policy-makers, and educators to engage in thoughtful examination of the sociocultural context in which African American and Latino youth live as they address their developmental and academic needs. The effectiveness of policy and the success of prevention and intervention programs depends upon continued research and dialogue which is thoughtful of and sensitive to the sociocultural characteristics of these youth, their families and communities.

References

Markus, H., & Nurius, P. (1986). Possible selves. *American Psychologist, 41*, 954–969.

Phelan, P., Davidson, A. L., & Yu, H. C. (1996). *Adolescents' worlds: Negotiating family, peers, and school.* New York: Teachers College Press.

Spencer, M. B. (1999). Social and cultural influences on school adjustment: The application of an identity-focused ecological perspective. *Educational Psychologist, 34*, 43–57.

Applied Developmental Science
2002, Vol. 6, No. 2, 62–72

Dreams of the Future: The Pursuit of Education and Career Possible Selves Among Ninth Grade Latino Youth

Constance M. Yowell

University of Illinois-Chicago

To better inform educational policies for Latino students, this study explores the relations between Latino students' conceptions of their futures and their risk status for school dropout. Using the theory of possible selves, the study examines students' hoped-for, expected, and feared selves, the power of those selves to predict risk status for school dropout, and the content of their specificity and ideological beliefs. Four hundred fifteen ninth grade Latino students were surveyed, 30 who also participated in interviews. Results indicated that Latino students' possible selves differed significantly, with hoped-for selves representing the highest levels of educational and occupational attainment. Although hoped-for and expected selves did not predict students' academic performance, feared selves did. The interviews indicated that the specificity and ideological beliefs housed within possible selves might be integral to the mechanisms through which those selves influence academic performance. The implications of the study's findings for school reform policies, specifically those advocating standardized assessments, are discussed.

A report commissioned by the Department of Education described current rates of school dropout among Latino students as "a shocking state of affairs" that risks the nation's economic and social systems, and the future lives and dreams of Latino youth. Rates of Latino dropout nationwide are approximately 35%, and typically are much higher in urban areas. Although dropout rates for African American and White students have declined recently, the dropout rate of Latino students has held steady over the past 25 years.

Research on student dropout and academic achievement has found causal relations between student expectations and educational outcomes. Consequently, many educational policies aimed at reducing dropout rates have been grounded, in part, in the assumption that students' expectations for school success and their academic achievement are related. Although expectations may play a crucial role in determining students' academic outcomes, this relationship is little understood. Furthermore, recent research has suggested that associations between expectations and academic outcomes may function differently for ethnic minority students than for middle-class White students. Such discrepancies in research findings suggest that before implementing policies grounded in an assumed association between expectations and academic outcomes, it may be nec-

essary to explore the role conceptions of the future may play in Latino students' school dropout.

Grounded in the theory of possible selves, this study explored the relations amongst ninth grade Latino students' conceptions of their possible futures and their risk status for school dropout. In addition, to better understand the mechanisms through which Latino students' conceptions of the future may influence their risk status for school dropout, the study also explored the ideological content and specificity of those conceptions. I begin with an overview of empirical studies examining the relations among student expectations and academic outcomes. Following this overview I outline the theoretical framework and hypotheses of the study.

Student Conceptions of the Future

Studies of academic achievement have consistently demonstrated that children's hopes or aspirations for future academic success are among the strongest predictors of school achievement. In an analysis of the 1992 NEXLS data, for example, Rigsby, Stull, and Morse-Kelly (1997) found that among Latino students, the strongest predictor of math achievement was students' expected years of schooling. Furthermore, Buriel and Cardoza (1988) found that the strongest predictor of Latino student achievement was neither generational status, socioeconomic status, nor Spanish language background, but was students' personal aspirations.

Requests for reprints should be sent to Constance M. Yowell, University of Illinois-Chicago

College of Education (M/C 147), 1040 West Harrison Street, Chicago, IL 60607–7133. E-mail: Connie@UIC.edu

Consistent with such findings, educational policies and practices have sought to increase student expectations for academic success in the hope of decreasing rates of school dropout. Programs such as "I Have a Dream," statewide policies to create a self-esteem curricula, and the inclusion in state goals or standards of statements such as "all students can go to college" ground their initiatives in the understanding that student aspirations significantly influence educational attainment. Similarly, a recent evaluation of dropout prevention programs for Latino students argued that successful "programs for disadvantaged youth must include those that aim to enhance the relevance of school to students' future" (Hispanic Dropout Project, 1998, p. 60).

Despite the apparent consistency in the research findings and the certainty of policymakers in legislating policies and programs aimed at enhancing student expectations, it is not clear that expectations or aspirations[1] for educational or economic success serve the same function for students of color as they may for middle-class White students. Cook, Church, Ajanaku, Kim, & Cohen (1996), for example, have shown that although the aspirations and expectations of middle-class White students typically are identical, African American students often demonstrate an aspirations–expectations gap in which aspirations are significantly higher than expectations. Furthermore, in contrast to studies detailing the strong association between student expectations and academic achievement, recent research has also shown that in the context of low academic achievement, students of color may continue to hold high expectations for future academic and career success. Research finding weak relations between expectations and achievement or an aspirations–expectations gap among students of color raise the question of whether student expectations for future educational or occupation success function differently for students of ethnic minority status than for middle-class White students.

To address this question, and to better inform educational policies and practices, this study used possible selves theory to explore the relations among the future orientations and academic achievement of Latino students. The theory provides distinctions among students' various conceptions of their future (i.e., hopes, expectations, fears), and it suggests mechanisms through which those conceptions may influence behavioral adaptation.

---

[1]Definitions of expectations and aspirations vary. In some studies "aspirations" and "expectations" may be used interchangeably to refer to an individual's hopes or dreams for the future. In other cases these concepts may represent the distinction between an individual's hopes or dreams (i.e., aspirations) for the future and an individual's understanding of what is most likely to happen in their future (i.e., expectations).

Future Orientation and the Theory of Possible Selves

Theorists have varied in their understanding of the nature of the temporal aspect of the self. Variously labeled identity formation, a motive, or a cognitive schema, time perspective has traditionally been considered integral to understanding goal directed behavior. More recent, personality theorists have sought to create middle level units of analyses that both take into account the autobiographies, projects, or concerns that give meaning to daily life and can be concretized with reference to daily activities. Theorists have posited that the meaning and relevance of pursuing daily goals draw explicitly from forward-oriented aspects of individuals' personal scripts, stories, or mental models of possible futures. Variously labeled "life tasks," or "possible selves," these cognitive-motivational theories presume complex relations between multiple and imaginative self-identities and purposive behavior.

At the core of several of these theories is the tendency to distinguish between individuals' representations of their current or now self, and representations of valued or feared or both end states. The former refers to one's self-concept while the latter may refer to one's self-guides or possible selves. Markus et al., in focusing on potential or possible selves, have hypothesized that one's subjective understanding of the future serves as the link or bridge between one's current self-concept and one's behavioral adaptation. According to Markus and Nurius (1996), the family of possible selves represents what persons would like to become—"hoped-for selves," what persons could become—"expected selves," and what persons are afraid of becoming—"feared selves." The theory of possible selves is especially useful for this investigation because it outlines mechanisms through which students' self-beliefs concerning their futures may serve to regulate patterns of school dropout, and it provides conceptual distinctions between the phenomena of aspirations and expectations.

According to possible selves theory, hoped-for selves, like aspirations, consist primarily of abstract wishes or fantasies, are grounded in little concrete knowledge of the means to achieve those fantasies, and have little connection to behavior. Conversely, expected selves are critical to behavioral adaptation because they contain the concrete scripts, strategies, plans, and affect for goal actualization. For expected selves to influence behavior, they must become increasingly concrete and contain specific plans and strategies for goal achievement (i.e., procedural knowledge). Furthermore, possible selves theory suggests that negative or feared selves are instrumental in the maintenance and direction of behavioral adaptation. Markus et al. suggest that while feared selves may not serve to organized and energize activity, they may function to guide avoidance behavior, thereby balancing the expected self. Thus, the theory of possible selves suggests that hoped-for, expected, and feared selves are conceptually distinct, with expected selves housing more specific procedural knowledge (i.e., scripts or plans) and therefore more likely to influence behavioral adaptation than hoped-for or feared selves.

Consistent with this theoretical framework, it was hypothesized that Latino students' expected selves would include more specific procedural knowledge related to goal attainment than either hoped-for or feared selves. It was further hypothesized that in light of this specificity, expected selves would be more likely to predict students' risk status for school dropout than would either hoped-for or feared selves.

The study also posited that the ideological content of possible selves might be a critical factor in determining the relations among Latino students' conceptions of their future and their risk status for school dropout. Mickelson (1990), for example, has suggested that the aspirations–expectations gap typically found among African American students may be due, in part, to students holding conflicting ideological beliefs (or attitudes) concerning the value or significance of education. She argued that when exploring students' aspirations for the future, researchers typically measure students' internalization of ideological beliefs that "embody Protestant ethic's promise of schooling as a vehicle for success and upward mobility" (p. 45). Such beliefs are captured often in dominant notions of the "American dream," and typically contain the assumption of equal opportunity for upward mobility for all citizens. Given the prevalence of such ideological beliefs within dominate culture, and given the abstract nature of aspirations (or hoped-for selves), Mickelson argued that it is reasonable for students (regardless of ethnicity, gender, or class) to internalize high aspirations for future educational and occupational success.

Consistent with possible selves theory, Mickelson (1990) also argued that expectations (i.e., expected selves) represent those goals of students that are grounded in a concrete and personalized understanding of the resources and opportunities for upward mobility available within their immediate social context. Although it is probable that the immediate social context of middle-class White students contains the resources and opportunities necessary for the attainment of the "American dream," it is unlikely that such resources and opportunities are contained within the social context of low-income ethnic minority students (Ogbu, 1978). Thus, differences in the domain specific ideological content (i.e., students' understanding of the role of education in ensuring occupational success) of aspirations and expectations of students of color may be reflected in their holding conflicted attitudes or beliefs about the role of schooling in promoting success and upward mobility. That is, all students may hope or aspire to achieve the ideals embodied in the "American dream." Students of color, through observations and direct or indirect communications with parents or other adults in the community, may also understand the concrete consequences of biased opportunity structures and hold attitudes or beliefs acknowledging the expectation that their access to the "American dream" will be constrained. Therefore, it was hypothesized that Latino students' educational and occupational hoped-for selves would differ from expected selves in ideological content, and consequently hoped-for selves would represent higher levels of future educational and occupational attainment than would expected selves.

Method

This study used a mixed quantitative and qualitative design to explore the relations among Latino students' domain specific (i.e., educational and occupational) possible selves and their school engagement (i.e., risk status for school dropout). The study also explored the role of specificity and ideological content in those relations. Consistent with the work of Cooper et al., the study focused on a single population. Cooper et al. argued that studies comparing ethnic minority and middle-class White students often result in the inappropriate labeling of ethnic minority youth as deficient in development. As a response to such deficit oriented interpretations, Cooper et al. suggested that exploratory research should seek to emphasize studies of single populations, while comparison studies may benefit from broadening their focus to include three or more ethnic minority groups. Given the exploratory nature of the study, it was framed to focus on one population of ethnic minority youth – students of Mexican descent.

Consistent with the theoretical framework of the study, survey measures were designed to test the following hypotheses:

1. Students' hoped-for selves will represent significantly greater educational attainment than their expected or feared selves, and

2. Students' educational expected selves will predict students' risk status for school dropout, while educational hoped-for and feared selves will not. Exploratory in-depth interviews, conducted with a subset of the students surveyed, were designed to explore the specificity (i.e., detailed understanding of goal attainment strategies) and ideological content (i.e., understanding of the role of education in future success) of students' possible selves, thereby addressing the remaining two hypotheses:

3. Students' expected selves will contain significantly greater specificity of plans and strategies to fulfill their goals than hoped-for or feared selves, and

4. Students' hoped-for selves will be consistent with the American ideological understanding of education as the primary means to upward mobility, while students' expected selves will represent beliefs grounded in a more concrete understanding of limited opportunities for economic success regardless of educational attainment.

Participants

The participants of the survey consisted of all ninth grade students (N = 415, M age, 15.3 years) in a large urban high school in a midwestern city that was present on the day the survey was administered. Three weeks following the administration of the survey, all students from two of the school's regular ninth grade English classes (approximately 56 students) were invited to participate in an in-depth interview. All students who attended the English classes and returned signed parental permission slips were interviewed during the final month of their freshman year. In an effort to insure that students who were having difficulty with school participated in the interviews, researchers also attended Saturday morning detention periods. Students fulfilling their detention were invited to participate in the study. Those returning permission slips were also interviewed.

The survey sample consisted of 228 (55%) boys and 187 (45%) ninth grade girls. The student population in the high school is 98% Mexican, consequently all students in the sample identified as Mexican or Mexican American. The majority of students in the sample (n = 232, 56%) were second generation,[2] with the remaining students identifying as either first (n = 120, 29%) or third (n = 63, 15%) generation. Data reflecting students' socioeconomic status included student reports of parent education. According to these reports, 50% of students have parents with some elementary school education, 12% have parents who completed high school, and 30% of students did not know the level of their parents' educational attainment. According to the 1990 census, the per capita income for the community is $7,500 and approximately 70% of the adults within the community received less than a high school education, indicating a predominately low socioeconomic status for a large majority of the participants. Consistent with this assessment, 90% of the students attending the school receive reduced lunch.

Thirty students participated in interviews. Eighteen were girls and 12 boys (M age, 15.23 years). Students ranged in academic achievement from a grade point average of 5.00 (on a 5-point scale) to a grade point average of .77. Twenty-seven percent of students reported grades reflecting a grade point average of 3.5 or above, 40% reported grades reflecting a grade point average greater than 2.0 and less than 3.5, and 33% of students reported grades reflecting a grade point average below 2.0. Eleven students were interviewed while completing a detention period.

Survey Administration and Measures

Students completed the Thinking About Your Future survey in their classrooms under the supervision of a trained administrator. The administrator read instructions for completing the survey, and was present to answer questions. Students completed the survey in one 45 min session. The survey contained items measuring educational and occupational possible selves, risk status for school dropout, and background characteristics.

Educational and occupational possible selves. Students were provided with directions consistent with previous measures of possible selves.[3] Hoped-for selves were defined in terms of dreams or hopes for the future, "they are what you most wish you will do in your life." Expected selves were described as what an individual believes is most likely to happen in the future, "they are things that you think will really happen in your life." Last, feared selves were referred to as "the things you don't want to do or have happen to you in the future." Because outcomes for education are clearly delineated, measures for educational possible selves were closed ended.[4]

Although students' occupational goals are often assessed using closed ended inventory or checklist measures (Cook et al., 1996; Henderson, 1997), open ended items were used to measure occupational possible selves because little is known about the types of jobs Latino students may hope, expect, or fear. Students were asked to list the three jobs they most hope to have in the future, the three jobs they expect to have in the future, and the three jobs they most want to avoid having in the future. Because the study examined the connections between students' educational and occu-

---

[2]The definition of generational history used was as following: first generation—student and parent(s) were born in Mexico; second generation—student was born in the United States and at least one parent was born in Mexico; third generation—student and parent(s) were born in the United States).

---

[3]The prompts were similar to those used by Oyserman and Markus (1990a). The study differs, however, in the use of domain specific (i.e., educational and occupational possible selves) measures. The prompts of Oyserman and Markus elicited general possible selves, which were then coded by researchers. In this study, the prompts asked students to list domain specific possible selves.

[4]Example of closed ended measures for educational possible selves: The most schooling I hope to complete is (please check only *one*). There were seven possible responses: 10th or 11th grade; high school graduation ... graduate school (law school, medical school). To enable the comparison of means, the options for educational possible selves were scored on a scale from 1 (10th or 11th grade) to 7 (graduate school).

pational selves the careers identified were coded by research assistants according to their educational requirements.[5]

Risk status for school dropout. The 5-Flag Identification system developed by Crichlow and Vito (1989) was modified to determine categories of risk status for school dropout. According to Crichlow and Vito, flags are to be assigned when yearly attendance was below 82%; national percentile scores on standardized achievement tests were below 38% for math and below 37% for reading; 2 or more core courses were failed in the course of the year (English, math, social studies, science); 2 or more instructional days were lost due to suspension; or the student was 1 or more years older than the student average at the same grade level. Students are then ranked on a scale from 1 to 5, according to the number of flags they have received. For this study, students' rates of absenteeism, grades, and suspensions were collected from school records. Age was self-reported. Students' scores on national tests were not available, however, consequently students were ranked on a scale from 1 to 4.

Frequency distributions were run for students' scores on risk status for school dropout. Given the low number of students in the ninth grade receiving four flags ($n = 25$), t tests were run to determine if those students receiving four flags and those receiving three flags differed significantly according to gender, generational history, educational and occupational possible selves, and at-risk status. Because significant differences between students receiving four flags and those receiving three flags were not found on these variables, the two groups were combined to form the group of students at highest risk for school dropout. Of the ninth grade students, 36% ($n = 149$) were low risk, 22% ($n = 92$) medium risk, and 42% ($n = 174$) high risk.

Background characteristics. Student generational history was based on student's self-reported birthplace and that of their parents (see Footnote 2). Students reported the educational levels of their mother and father. Levels were scored on a scale from 1 (some elementary school) to 7 (graduate school). Scores were then averaged to form the parent education variable.

Student Interviews

Following the administration of the survey, members of the research team visited the two English classes to describe the in-depth interviews and invite students to participate. As students returned parental permission slips, they were interviewed either during a free period during the school day, or on Saturday morning. All interviews were conducted in private spaces in the school and were audiotaped. The interviews ranged from 40 to 90 min, with the average interview lasting approximately 60 min.

The interviews explored the specific plans, strategies, or schema attached to students' hoped-for, expected, and feared selves. The section of the interview reported here[6] consisted of three primary questions, with each question comprised of a series of probes. First, the content of students' possible selves was explored. Students were reminded of the survey they had recently taken. Students were not shown the survey they had completed, instead they were asked to recall their responses to specific survey questions. Students recalled their survey responses with 87% accuracy. Students were also given an opportunity to add new possible selves if they desired.

Second, students were asked questions concerning their strategies for achieving their hoped-for and expected selves (e.g., "What do you think you will need to do to go to college, graduate from high school, etc. ..."; "What do you think you may need to do to reach your [specific career] goals?"). Students were also asked to describe a scenario in which their feared selves may be realized and how such a scenario may be avoided.

Third, grounded in the work of Mickelson (1990), a series of questions explored students' ideological beliefs concerning their possible selves (e.g., "What do you need to do to be a success?"; "Do you think your parents have had a fair chance at getting a good job?"; "Do you think you will have a fair chance at getting a good job?"). Interviews were coded for specificity and consistency with dominant American ideological beliefs concerning the means and potential access to upward mobility. Because understandings of educational and occupational success were considerably intertwined, only one specificity and one ideological score were coded per possible self for each participant. Specificity was rated on a scale from one to three, increasing as students' descriptions of plans and strategies for fulfilling their hoped-for and expected selves and avoiding their feared selves increased.[7]

---

[6]See Yowell (in press) for a more detailed discussion of additional interview questions and analyses.

[7]Hoped-for and Expected Selves were coded according to the following protocol:

1 Participant stated a general plan or strategy necessary to achieve the self (e.g.,"I hope to get a good job so I will have to do well in school").

2 Participant stated a general plan or strategy, and at least one specific component of a strategy to achieve self (e.g., "I want to be a teacher ... I will need to go to college"; "I can take courses at the community college next to my house to be a computer programmer").

---

[5]Occupational selves were scored on a scale from 1 (*doesn't require a high school diploma*) to 7 (*occupation requires a graduate school degree*).

Ideological scores for hoped-for and expected selves were dichotomous to signify the presence or absence of an understanding of unequal educational or occupational opportunities (e.g., unequal access to the "American dream"). Hoped-for or expected selves were scored a two if students discussed beliefs that were specific to their social context or indicated an unequal opportunity for success based on their immigrant, ethnic, or gender status (e.g., "even if I do well in school I might not get a good job"; "my parents tell me its going to be hard for me to get a job because I am Mexican"; " my parents don't have a fair chance at getting a good job because they weren't born here"). Students' received a code of one if they described their hoped-for or expected selves in terms of ideological beliefs consistent with the "American dream" (e.g., "if I work hard in school I will be a success in my career"; "if I do well in school I will be able to do better than my parents").

Coders for both specificity and ideological beliefs were blind to the identity of the participants. One-third of the interviews were given specificity and ideological belief ratings by two coders jointly. These coders demonstrated a 94% inter-rater reliability for specificity and a 100% inter-rater reliability for ideological beliefs. A single coder was responsible for rating the specificity and ideological beliefs of the remaining interviews.

Results

Content of Educational and Occupational Possible Selves

To explore Hypothesis 1, separate repeated measures analyses of variance with covariates (ANCOVAs) were

---

3 Participant stated a general plan or strategy, outlined at least two critical steps necessary to achieve self, stated an obstacle and a strategy for overcoming it (e.g., "I'm going to be an architect, so I'm going to work on my drawing in high school, and then I'll go to college and be an architecture major in college ... but money might be a problem ... so maybe I will apply for scholarships").

Feared Selves were coded according to the following protocol:

1 Participants identified a fear and a reason for the fear (e.g., "I'm afraid I won't finish high school ... because I don't do my homework").

2 Participant identified a scenario in which feared self might come true, and its consequences ("I'm afraid I'll drop out of high school ... sometimes you get so far behind that's its impossible to make it up ... so you stop coming ... then its hard to get a good job").

3 Participant stated a scenario in which the feared self might come true, its consequences, and identified a strategy for avoiding the feared self, (e.g., "I'm afraid I might become pregnant ... if you start dating a boy and they want to its hard to say no ... and then I couldn't finish high school ... so I'm not going to start dating until I'm in college").

performed for the educational and occupational domains. These ANCOVAS were used to determine if hoped-for, expected, and feared selves differed significantly. The dependent variables were hoped-for, expected, and feared selves within the educational and occupational domains, and the covariates were gender and generational history. These two variables were chosen as covariates because considerable research (Romo & Falbo, 1996; Suarez-Orozco & Suarez-Orozco, 1995) has suggested that Latino students' risk status for school dropout differs significantly by gender (i.e., boys demonstrate typically a higher dropout rate than girls) and generational history (i.e., second and third generation students show typically higher dropout rates than first generation students).

The first repeated measures ANCOVA revealed that students' educational possible selves differed significantly, $F(2, 404) = 15.43$, $p < .001$ (see Table 1). Follow up comparisons using Tukey's HSD procedure indicated that students' educational hoped-for selves were significantly higher than their expected and feared selves ($p < .01$). Similarly, educational expected selves were also significantly higher than students' feared selves ($p < .01$). Confirming Hypothesis 1, these differences indicated that hoped-for, expected, and feared selves each represented significantly differing conceptions of educational attainment.

Covariate coefficients revealed a significant relationship between the covariates of gender and generational history and the dependent variables of educational hoped-for, $F(2, 404) = 3.30$, $p < .05$ and expected selves $F(2, 404) = 2.72$, $p < .05$. The covariate coefficients revealed ($p < .05$) that first generation students held significantly higher hoped-for and expected educational selves than did second or third generation students.

Similarly confirming Hypothesis 1, the second repeated measures ANCOVA revealed differences among occupational possible selves. The top five most commonly identified hoped-for occupations (e.g., doctor, lawyer, computer programmer) required a college education, while the top five expected occupations varied from requiring a college degree to not requiring high school graduation (e.g., teacher, police officer, secretary). Students, however, were consistent in reporting occupational feared selves that did not require high school graduation (e.g., factory or fast food worker, janitor).

Not surprising, these occupational possible selves differed significantly in their educational requirements $F(2, 404) = 12.78$, $p < .001$. Follow up comparisons using Tukey's HSD procedure indicated that students' occupational hoped-for selves required significantly higher educational attainment than their expected selves ($p < .01$), and that both hoped-for and expected selves required significantly higher educational attainment than students' feared selves ($p < .01$) (see Table

Table 1. *Frequency of Students' Hoped-For, Expected, and Feared Selves by Domain*

Educational Level	Educational Domain			Occupational Domain		
	Hoped-For Selves (%)	Expected Selves (%)	Feared Selves (%)	Hoped-For Selves (%)	Expected Selves (%)	Feared Selves (%)
High School Dropout	2.10	30.60	31.90	21.20	36.10	77.30
High School Graduate	15.30	8.30	43.20	7.30	10.80	6.80
Vocational Training	5.70	14.20	3.40	21.50	18.20	3.30
Complete Some College	12.90	42.10	14.80	NA	NA	NA
Community College	10.20	1.40	5.20	7.40	6.70	3.20
4-Year University	46.30	6.30	4.30	22.70	20.40	8.80
Graduate School	10.10	1.20	NA	22.30	11.20	NA
M	5.00	3.38	2.53	4.17	3.32	1.82
SD	1.69	1.85	1.58	2.27	2.25	1.74

1). Thus, the findings for the repeated measures ANCOVAs were consistent with previous research suggesting that ethnic minority students may report an aspirations–expectations gap in which aspirations were significantly greater than expectations. According to Hypothesis 2, these differing possible selves should also demonstrate differences in their power to predict students' risk status for school dropout.

Possible Selves and Risk Status for School Dropout.

Six multiple regression analyses were performed to determine the unique role of each educational and occupational possible self in predicting Latino students' risk status for school dropout. In each equation risk status for school dropout was the dependent variable, and one of the six separate occupational or educational possible selves (i.e., hoped-for, expected or feared selves within two domains) was an independent variable. In addition, background characteristics such as parental education, gender (males coded as 0 and females as 1), and generational history (first generation coded as 0; third generation coded as 2) were entered into each equation as independent variables. The alpha level for the regression equations was adjusted to $p < .008$ using the Bonferroni technique to control for Type I error. All six equations were found to be significant. In contrast to Hypothesis 2, only the equation with educational feared selves revealed a measure of possible selves that significantly contributed to the prediction of risk status $F(5, 405) = 8.88, p < .0001, r = .47$.

In addition to educational feared selves, student gender and generational history significantly contributed to patterns of risk status for school dropout (see Table 2). Male students were more likely to be at risk for dropout than female students. Similarly, second and third generation students were more likely to be at high risk for school dropout than were first generation students. The negative sign for educational feared selves indicated that the more students feared low edu-

cational outcomes (e.g., school dropout) the more likely they were to actually be at risk for dropout.

Specificity and Ideology of Possible Selves

To explore Hypothesis 3, a repeated measures ANOVA was used to determine if the interviewed students differed in the specificity of their descriptions of possible selves. The study posited that expected selves would predict students' risk status for school dropout because, in part, those selves housed procedural knowledge for future goal attainment that was greater in specificity than plans and strategies housed within hoped-for selves. The findings indicated that students' specificity in their descriptions of hoped-for ($M = 1.33$, $SD = .60$), expected ($M = .43, SD = .68$), and feared ($M = 2.27, SD = .74$) selves did vary significantly $F(2, 29) = 55.42, p < .001$. Failing to confirm Hypothesis 3, however, follow up comparisons using Tukey's HSD procedure revealed that the specificity of students' expected selves was not significantly greater than the specificity of their hoped-for selves. The specificity of feared selves, however, was significantly greater than that of either hoped-for or of expected selves ($p < .01$).

As shown in Table 3, the limited difference in specificity between hoped-for and expected selves was due primarily to students' vague and general descriptions

Table 2. *Summary of Regression Analyses for Variables Predicting Risk Status for School Dropout (N = 415)*

Variable	β	T
Gender	−0.152*	−2.33
Generational History	0.201*	2.07
Parent Education	0.064	0.78
Educational Hoped-For Self	−0.061	−0.95
Educational Expected Self	−0.043	−1.15
Educational Feared Self	−0.311**	−4.51
Occupational Hoped-For Self	−0.048	−0.73
Occupational Expected Self	−0.015	−1.50
Occupational Feared Self	−0.118	−1.36

*$p < .01$. **$p < .001$

Table 3. *Frequency of Specificity and Student Descriptions of Possible Selves*

Specificity Code	Possible Self, Frequency of Specificity, and Description
3	*Hoped-For,* ($n = 2/7\%$): "the most important hope for me is to finish high school so I could become a dentist. I'm getting a lot of knowledge of science in biology, and medicine too. I have to finish high school, then college, then medical school. I go to a program on Saturdays to make sure I keep my grades and learn what I need to learn."
	Expected, ($n = 3/10\%$): "My brother is an electrician. I'll probably do that. I'll need to finish high school. There's a school he went to for a couple of years to train."
	Fear, ($n = 13/43\%$): "I don't wanna think about not finishing high school—that's my biggest fear, because then I would get a job at McDonald's. Right now I have friends I see and I don't wanna be that. That's what makes me want to study more."
2	*Hoped-For,* ($n = 6/20\%$) : "I want to finish high school when I'm 18 … and then I hope to go to college for a couple of years … for three years, no for two years. I don't know, how many credits you need in college? … I just hope to get to there."
	Expected, ($n = 7/23\%$): "I hope to be a lawyer, but what I'll probably do is design clothes … I'll have to finish high school and then take classes that will train me…"
	Fear, ($n = 12/40\%$): "my brother was in a gang. He was in a crew and he been in jail for doing stupid things. I see what it did to him and my parents …I just see them and I see him and it makes me think I can't do this to my parents too …"
1	*Hoped-For,* ($n = 22/73\%$): "I hope to be a doctor … first, I need to get my education … all that the school is giving out, I think I'll need it."
	Expected, ($n = 20/67\%$): "In order to complete high school. I need to work harder … then I'll be fine"
	Fear, ($n = 5 /17\%$): "I think its going to get hard but I don't want to give up because I really want to become a nurse. That's what I'm afraid of, that its going to get harder and I'll give up in school"

of plans for the attainment of hoped-for or expected selves. The majority of students received low specificity scores (i.e., a score of 1) for both hoped-for ($n = 22$, 73%) and expected selves ($n = 20$, 67%) because they provided general descriptions of a linear connection between hard work, education, and occupational success. Students' primary strategy for ensuring success was to "work harder." On occasion, students identified technical tasks necessary for the completion of high school such as "turning in homework assignments," "stop cutting so many classes" or simply "make sure I get all my credits." Given the theoretical premise of the study, the finding of expected selves housing procedural knowledge marked by limited specificity may provide insight into the limited association between expected selves and risk status for school dropout.

More interesting, students were significantly more specific in descriptions of feared selves. Students' feared selves included engagement in activities that would lead to negative consequences or failure to attain an expected or hoped-for self. Students described in detail experiences of friends and family members that represented engagement in risk activities (e.g., pregnancy, gang violence, drug use, school dropout), and the consequences of such actions. Students were less successful (those coded as 1 or 2, $n = 17$), however, in describing strategies for avoiding feared selves, relying on "hard work," and "just don't do it," as strategies for avoidance. Such specificity may be a critical determinant in understanding the role of feared selves in predicting Latino students' risk status for school dropout.

Ideological beliefs were consistent across all 30 students: All students interviewed articulated an understanding and a clear belief in the role of schooling and hard work in achieving the "American dream." Consistent with dominate notions of how to achieve the "American dream," all students clearly articulated a linear relationship between education and economic success (e.g., "you have to go to college to get a good job"; "… to be a success I have to work, do well in school, and then I'll get a good job"), and all students clearly described hard work as the central strategy or cause of success (e.g., "if I try hard I will be successful"). Furthermore, students interviewed did not articulate an understanding of future advancement that would contradict dominate ideological beliefs concerning equal access to opportunity for all groups and individuals in the United States. No student, for example, stated a belief (or a message communicated from a parent) that they would receive fewer economic opportunities because of their gender, ethnicity, or immigrant status, or that their educational success may not ensure their upward mobility. In additional, while the majority of the students (73%) identified a personal weakness (e.g., laziness, not smart enough) as a possible reason for failure in the future, no student indicated that the school system, the economic structure, or limited opportunities and resources available within their community represented obstacles to their occupational success.

Discussion

The study examined ninth grade Latino students' possible selves, the specificity, and ideological content of domain specific possible selves, and the associations between those possible selves and risk for school dropout. It was hypothesized that hoped-for selves, grounded in abstract ideological beliefs, would represent higher levels of educational and occupational attainment than would expect selves. It was also hypothesized that expected selves, embedded in concrete and specific personal realities rather than dominate ideological beliefs about social mobility, would represent lower levels of educational and occupational achievement and would more accurately predict Latino students' risk for school dropout than would hoped-for selves.

Consistent with these hypotheses a hoped-for–expected selves gap emerged within the educational and occupational domains. Students' identified higher levels of attainment for hoped-for selves than for their expected selves. This hoped-for–expected selves gap suggests that students' expected selves might be more consistent with the realities of social context, while the content of hoped-for selves may be ideologically consistent with dreams of educational and occupational success. Because no relations were found among occupational possible selves and students' risk for school dropout, the remainder of the discussion will be limited to the findings concerning educational possible selves. Research suggests that occupational expectations have, at best, only an indirect effect on student outcomes. Because students' conceptions of their careers typically do not become salient identity issues until students begin to make career choices, such effects emerge often in late, rather than early or middle, adolescence.

In contrast to the study's hypotheses, domain specific hoped-for and expected selves did not differ in specificity, ideological content, or in their association with risk status for school dropout. Previous studies have argued that the limited association between expectations and educational outcomes for students of color may be due to expectations that are inappropriately high given academic achievement. The hoped-for–expected selves gap indicates, however, that students surveyed recognize both dreams of achievement and the possibility of limited educational and occupational success. A critical variable for these students may be found in the limited specificity of the procedural knowledge housed within both hoped-for and expected selves. Students' understanding of how to achieve their dreams and their more tempered expectations were vague and abstract, and did not differ in ideological content. In fact, the procedural knowledge of both hoped-for and expected selves consisted primarily of an ideological understanding of the relations between individual hard work, educational attainment, and social mobility. It may be that the absence of procedural knowledge undermines the role of hoped-for and expected selves in organizing and energizing behavior. Thus, given the absence of specificity, it is not inconsistent with the theory of possible selves that both educational hoped-for and expected selves were ineffective in predicting students' risk for school dropout.

In contrast to hoped-for and expected selves, students' feared selves did predict their risk status for school dropout. Students' fears were embedded in strong visual imagery and affect, an understanding of how their fears may be actualized, and recognition of the consequences of such actualization. More interesting, the procedural knowledge housed within students' feared selves was consistent with a theoretical understanding of the specificity that ought to be housed within expected selves. It may be such specificity that explains the role of students' educational feared selves in predicting risk status for school dropout.

Alternatively, it may also be the case that students feel more comfortable providing socially undesirable responses to items measuring feared selves than they do items measuring expected selves. Given students' ideological understanding of the pathways to economic success, it may be both socially undesirable and psychologically threatening to acknowledge an educational expected self that includes school dropout. Regardless of the social desirability of student responses, however, the interviews indicated that even in the context of lowered expectations (e.g., high school graduation or matriculation to community college) students' understanding of the processes or steps necessary to fulfill such goals was limited.

The findings may provide insight into both the mechanisms underlying school engagement and the types of support, guidance, and information Latino students may receive within their home and educational contexts. The absence of concrete and personalized procedural knowledge within expected selves, in the context of well defined feared selves, may have critical consequences for students' school engagement. According to possible selves theory, although procedural knowledge housed within expected selves guides behavior, feared selves do little more than guide avoidance behaviors. In the absence of delineated expected selves, students may drift or randomly engage those behaviors that are the most clearly defined (in this case feared selves). According to possible selves theory, the lack of balance between detailed and personalized expected and feared selves may compromise the school engagement and outcomes of Latino youth.

The content and specificity of students' expected and feared selves suggests that while the educational and social context may provide information and experiences concerning behaviors that students ought to avoid and ideological beliefs to internalize, little meaningful information may be provided concerning strategies necessary for school engagement. That is, although students clearly understand the associations between certain risk taking behaviors (e.g., pregnancy and gang activity) and school failure, they were able to identify only broad ideological outlines of relations between high school graduation, college matriculation, and social mobility. The findings concerning the imbalance between expected and feared selves, the limited procedural knowledge housed within expected selves, and the lack of association between expectations and risk status for school dropout raise several issues to be considered in the development of programs and policies aimed at reducing the dropout rates of Latino students.

Implications for Programs and Policies

This study highlights the importance of developing dropout prevention initiatives, curricula, or guidance counseling programs that engage Latino students in meaningful and realistic discussions of their possible futures. It is common for current intervention programs to focus either on the negative consequences of certain behaviors (e.g., Reducing the Risk and D.A.R.E. are sex education and drug prevention programs whose goal is to prevent adolescent involvement in sexual or drug related activities) or on raising the self-esteem and expectations of students (e.g., California Task Force on Self-Esteem was established to create policies for the state that would increase students' self esteem and by extension their test scores). It may be the case that rather than emphasizing negative or positive performance outcomes of students, policies, and programs must first focus on creating contexts for students that allow for engagement in activities and discussions that build meaningful connections between present context and expectations for the future.

Within the context of urban high schools two programmatic responses to students may serve to undermine the building of such connections: (a) high school guidance counseling practices, and (b) an increased emphasis on student assessment. Research on the role of guidance counseling in preparing youth for their futures has noted that many counselors take the "college for all" approach to guidance. Rather than prepare students for realistic futures, counselors seek to protect the ego and self-esteem of their students. Rosenbaum et al. argued that the challenge for guidance counselors is to commit neither "sins of omission"—allowing students to believe in unrealistic expectations, nor "sins of commission"—telling students they can not go to college, but to provide students with accurate and sensitive feedback concerning their current performance while offering the guidance and information necessary for goal attainment.

Although high schools traditionally have left the provision of such procedural knowledge to parents, the findings suggest that in the context of low income and ethnic minority communities, access to such knowledge may be extremely limited. Therefore it becomes the responsibility of educational institutions to offer students experiences that not only provide meaningful information and feedback, but also engage students in thoughtful critique of how dominate ideological beliefs may or may not accurately represent strategies for and access to social mobility within the United States.

The results also indicate that embedded in the ideological content and procedural knowledge of students' possible selves is an understanding of education as a purely functional endeavor. Although students interviewed clearly described the significance of educational credentials for their futures, no student discussed the significance of subject matter knowledge or learning more generally, and no student associated educational experiences with individual growth. Rather, students described worries related to test performance, and the significance of such performances for their advancement to the next grade level. Such descriptions document the success of the current standards movement to equate learning and the purpose of schooling with assessment.[8] From the perspective of students, the danger of such an equation may be the elimination of educational contexts that support intrinsic motivation. Furthermore, the linking of students' educational futures with the press for improved outcomes on standardized tests may be translated in the classroom and understood by students as a search for the right answer. Such high stakes and functional understanding of learning may undermine attempts to foster creative and critical thinking skills necessary to enact the steps or strategies for goal attainment and personal growth. Thus, the role of assessment policies in influencing students' understanding of procedural knowledge and pursuit of hoped-for and expected selves is clearly a question for greater empirical analysis.

Similarly, in further research it will be important to include a broader analysis of the relations among procedural knowledge, educational outcomes, social context, and development. It is unclear, for example, to what extent the abstract nature of students' procedural knowledge is a function of maturity, and will develop over the course of students' high school experience. In further research, longitudinal studies may answer such questions.

It should also be noted that the findings related to specificity and ideology are based on a small number of in-depth interviews, and must be considered highly tentative and exploratory. Despite the tentative nature of the findings, however, the uniformity of students' ideological beliefs related to schooling is noteworthy. Although previous research has interpreted differences in academic outcomes between first and second or third generation Latino students in the context of famil-

---

[8]It should be noted that the study was conducted in a midwestern city whose recent educational policy initiatives have emphasized student assessments. In the past two years the school system has mandated that students' scores on standardized tests be used to determine both grade level promotion and graduation.

ial or student perceptions of the value of schooling, the uniformity found in this study may suggest that factors other than ideological beliefs may be contributing to the disparity among generational groups. It is possible, for example, that the results represent a selection bias. Perhaps those Latino families that become prosperous choose to leave low income urban areas, potentially reducing the number of second and third generation students who perform well in school.

Alternatively, such uniformity in students' responses may represent methodological issues that require further unraveling. The interview protocol was consistent with research conducted within primarily African American populations (Mickelson, 1990), and may not facilitate adequately discussions of access to opportunity among Latino populations. Students, for example, were not asked explicitly if they believed subpopulations might experience unequal access to opportunities for social mobility. Rather, more indirect, but personal questions signifying such a belief were used. Such an approach may have influenced the ideological content of student responses, and must be explored further.

In addition, the factors contributing to the risk status of male Latino students require greater examination. Research has indicated that gang activity, urban poverty, and familial norms for the early entry of men into the labor force may significantly influence the educational outcomes of male Latino students. In further studies, it will be important to include more culturally specific items that reflect the varying ideological beliefs and procedural knowledge of Latino students, and to examine in more depth the role of social context variables in shaping the educational pathways of Latino youth.

References

Alexander, K., Entwisle, D., & Bedinger, S. (1994). When expectations work: Race and socioeconomic differences in school performance. *Social Psychology Quarterly, 57,* 283–299.

Buriel, R., & Cardoza, D. (1988). Sociocultural correlates of achievement among three generations of Mexican American high school seniors. *American Educational Research Journal, 25,* 177–192.

Cantor, N., & Zirkel, S. (1990). Personality, cognition, and purposive behavior. In L. Pervin (Eds.), *Handbook of personality: Theory and research* (pp. 135–164). New York: Guilford Press.

Coleman, J., Ernest, C., Hobson, C., McPartland, J., Mood, A., Weinfeld, D., & York, R. (1966). *Equality of Educational Opportunity.* Washington, DC: U.S. Government Printing Office.

Cook, T., Church, M., Ajanaku, S., Kim, J. R., & Cohen, R. (1996). The development of occupational aspirations and expectations among inner-city boys. *Child Development, 67,* 3368–3385.

Cooper, C., Jackson, J., Azmitia, M., & Lopez, E. (1998). Multiple selves, multiple worlds: Three useful strategies for research with ethnic minority youth on identity, relationships, and opportunity structures. In V. McLoyd & L. Steinberg (Eds.), *Studying minority adolescents: Conceptual, methodological, and theoretical issues* (pp. 111–127). Mahwah, NJ: Lawrence Erlbaum Associates, Inc.

Darling-Hammond, L., & Wise, A. E. (1985). Beyond standardization: State standards and school improvement. *Elementary School Journal, 85,* 315–336.

Deci, E., & Ryan, R. (1985). *Intrinsic motivation and self-determination in human behavior.* New York: Plenum Press.

Erikson, E. H. (1964). *Insight and responsibility.* New York: W.W. Norton.

Gamoran, A. (1987). The stratification of high school learning opportunities. *Sociology of Education, 60,* 135–155.

Henderson, R. W. (1997). Educational and occupational aspirations and expectations among parents of middle school students of Mexican descent: Family resources for academic development and mathematics learning. In R. W. Taylor & M. C. Wang (Eds.), *Social and emotional adjustment and family relations in ethnic minority families* (pp. 99–131). Mahwah, NJ: Lawrence Erlbaum Associates, Inc.

Hispanic Dropout Project (1998). *No more excuses: The final report of the Hispanic dropout project.* Washington, DC: U.S. Department of Education.

Isreali, N. (1936). *Abnormal personality and time.* New York: Science Press.

Kastenbaum, R. (1964). The structure and function of time perspectives. *Journal of Psychological Research, 8,* 1–11.

MacLeod, J. (1987). *Ain't no makin' it: Leveled aspirations in a low-income neighborhood.* Boulder, CO: Westview Press.

Marin, G., & Marin, B. V. (1991). *Research with Hispanic populations.* London: Sage.

Markus, H., & Nurius, P. (1986). Possible selves. *American Psychologist, 41,* 954–969.

Mickelson, R. A. (1990). The attitude-achievement paradox among Black adolescents. *Sociology of Education, 63,* 44–61.

Ogbu, J., 1978. *Minority education and caste: The American system in cross-cultural perspective.* New York: Academic Press.

Oyserman, D., & Markus, H. (1990a). Possible selves and delinquency. *Journal of Personality and Social Psychology, 59,* 112–125.

Oyserman, D., & Markus, H. (1990b). Possible selves in balance: Implications for delinquency. *Journal of Social Issues, 46,* 141–157.

Rigsby, L. C., Stull, J. C., & Morse-Kelley, N. (1997). Determinants of student educational expectations and achievement: Race/ethnicity and gender differences. In R. W. Taylor & M. C. Wang (Eds.), *Social and emotional adjustment and family relations in ethnic minority families* (pp. 201–227). Mahwah, NJ: Lawrence Erlbaum Associates, Inc.

Romo, H. D., & Falbo, T. (1996). *Latino high school graduation.* Austin, TX: University of Texas Press.

Rosenbaum, J., Miller, S., & Krei, M. (1996). Gatekeeping in an era of more open gates: High school counselor's views of their influence on students' college plans. *American Journal of Education, 104,* 257–279.

State of Illinois Board of Higher Education (1999). *The Illinois commitment: Partnerships, opportunities, and excellence.* Springfield, IL: State of Illinois Board of Higher Education.

Suarez-Orozco, C., & Suarez-Orozco, M. (1995). *Transformations: Migration, family life, and achievement motivation among Latino adolescents.* Stanford, CA: Stanford University Press.

Yowell, C. M. (in press). The role of the future in meeting the challenge of Latino school dropouts. *Educational Foundations.*

Received April 2, 1999
Final revision received July 9, 1999
Accepted July 28, 1999

Applied Developmental Science
2002, Vol. 6, No. 2, 73–87

Bridging Multiple Worlds: How African American and Latino Youth in Academic Outreach Programs Navigate Math Pathways to College

Catherine R. Cooper
University of California, Santa Cruz

Robert G. Cooper, Jr.
San Jose State University

Margarita Azmitia and Gabriela Chavira
University of California, Santa Cruz

Yvette Gullatt
University of California, Berkeley

Universities have launched outreach programs to enhance their ethnic diversity, yet little developmental research examines students' pathways to college. This study compares capital models (highlighting family background) with challenge models (highlighting students' challenges and resources) in predicting pathways to college. The Bridging Multiple Worlds Model frames this longitudinal study of 120 African American and Latino youth in outreach programs. We examined students' family backgrounds; challenges and resources across family, school, peer, and community worlds; and high school math pathways as predictors of college eligibility and enrollment. African American students more typically had U. S. born, college-educated parents, and Latino students, immigrant parents with high school education or less. Second, students saw parents as greater resources than teachers, siblings, and themselves; peers and teachers were their greatest challenges. Youth distinguished resources and challenges more by their source than form. Third, high school math and English grades rose and fell together, with early math grades predicting college eligibility. Five math pathways emerged: steady, slowly declining, rapidly declining, increasing, and "back on track" toward college, but pathways did not always predict college choices. Fourth, although family background predicted few outcomes, parents' and teachers' help and siblings' challenges predicted grades, eligibility, and admission to prestigious colleges. Findings highlight both capital and challenge models for science, policy, and programs involving diversity and equity.

This investigation was supported by a grant to C. R. Cooper, J. F. Jackson, and M. Azmitia from the University of California Linguistic Minority Research Institute. The project was also supported by the Institute of Human Development at the University of California, Berkeley; the Bilingual Research Center and the National Center for Research in Cultural Diversity and Second Language Learning at the University of California, Santa Cruz; and the John D. and Catherine T. MacArthur Foundation Research Network on Successful Pathways through Middle Childhood.

We thank our colleague Jacquelyne F. Jackson; our research staff, including Edward M. Lopez, Nora Dunbar, July Figueroa, Zena Mello, Teri Henson, Edna Rosales, Christine Smallwood, Jayme Barrett, David Cooper, Renee Ferigo Marshall, Lisa Fonseca, Conrad Amba, Christiane Gaulthier, Karen Godfredsen-Gomez, Alma Lopez, Mary Lucero, Laura Mayorga, Kate Perry, and Jennifer Selke; consultants Diana Baumrind and William Meredith; and colleagues Ron Gallimore, Patricia Gándara, Bud Mehan, and Barbara Rogoff. We also thank the students, families, and outreach program leadership, including Ben Tucker, Liz Chavez, and Tara Henry.

Requests for reprints should be sent to C. R. Cooper, Department of Psychology, Social Sciences 2, University of California, Santa Cruz, CA 95064. E-mail: ccooper@cats.ucsc.edu

In the United States, as each cohort of students moves through secondary school to college, the percentage of African American and Latino adolescents shrinks, a pattern that has become known as the *academic pipeline problem* (Gándara, Larson, Mehan, & Rumberger, 1998; Geiser, 1996). A key indicator of college eligibility, revealed in studies of nationally representative samples, is the sequence of math classes students take in high school. Asian American students take more advanced college-preparatory math than European American students, and both groups take more college-prep math than African American or Latino students (Catsambis, 1994; Davenport, Davison, Kuang, Ding, Kim, & Kwak, 1998). Research is moving beyond ethnic group differences to map variation within groups and similarities across them in conditions that enhance college and career choices of ethnically diverse students (Gándara, 1995).

California provides a key setting for investigating how African American and Latino youth navigate pathways to college. California law mandates that the top 12.5% of high school graduates be considered eligible for the University of California (UC), the top 33% eligible for the California State University System (CSU), and all 18-year-olds and all high school graduates eligible for the California Community College System. Yet in 1996, only 4.5% of African American and 3.5% of Latino high school graduates in California were eligible for UC, based on college-prep class grades and Scholastic Aptitude Test (SAT) scores (Edgert & Taylor, 1996). Moving beyond UC eligibility, the National Education Longitudinal Survey of 1988 (NELS:88), based on nationally representative cohorts of eighth grade students, showed that among California students, African American and Latino students were underrepresented among those in 4-year colleges and overrepresented among those who did not finish high school (Gándara et al., 1998).

When the University of California Board of Regents removed race and ethnicity as considerations in the admission of undergraduate students in 1996, university outreach programs took on a key role in strengthening diversity in California higher education (Hayward, Brandes, Kirst, & Mazzeo, 1997). These range from *competitive* programs, whose graduates typically attend UC or CSU, to *selective* programs whose graduates attend community college, from which they may qualify for 4-year institutions. Despite 30 years of outreach programs, however, little developmental research exists about successful pathways to college among participants.

This article reports findings from an ongoing research partnership with outreach programs that seek to provide bridges through school into college and college-based occupations (Cooper, Jackson, Azmitia, Lopez, & Dunbar, 1995; Cooper, Jackson, Azmitia, & Lopez, 1998). The study focuses on four questions: What were the family backgrounds of youth participating in these programs in terms of immigration history and parents' education? What resources and challenges did students experience from their families, peers, school, and communities? What were students' pathways through math classes required for university eligibility? And how did students' family backgrounds, resources and challenges across worlds, and high school math pathways predict college eligibility and enrollment?

In addressing these questions, we drew on three related models that move beyond ethnic group differences to understand how ethnically diverse youth and their relationships, institutions, and cultural communities interact and change over time. The first is Ecocultural Theory, which integrates ecological and cultural perspectives (Gallimore, Goldenberg, & Weisner, 1993; Rogoff, 1990; Weisner, Gallimore, &

Jordan, 1988). This theory assumes families in all cultural communities work to adapt to changing ecologies through their routines of everyday life. Culture is seen in the dimensions of these routines or *activity settings*, including their typical participants or *personnel*; the *values and beliefs* that give meaning to their lives; and the *scripts* or recurring patterns of communication (Reese, Gallimore, Goldenberg, & Balzano, 1995). Our study built on Ecocultural Theory by tracing the personnel and scripts of ethnically diverse youth who shared the value of attending college.

Our second theoretical perspective, the *Students' Multiple Worlds Model,* was proposed by educational anthropologists Phelan, Davidson, and Yu (1991) to learn how youth navigate across their family, peer, and school contexts. Phelan et al. used geographical metaphors of *world* to refer to the cultural knowledge and expectations held in each context and *navigation* to capture youth's experiences as they try moving across the borders between worlds. In a longitudinal study of California high school students selected to vary in ethnicity, gender, immigration history, and achievement, Phelan et al. found many students whose worlds differed in culture, ethnicity, social class, or religion. Some found crossing borders manageable while others found it difficult. The most vulnerable youth found borders between worlds impenetrable and became alienated from school. And crossing borders did not come without costs; students with bicultural identities were criticized by people in each world for being disloyal. Our study built on the Students' Multiple Worlds Model by adding outreach programs as a key world and a developmental focus to trace how experiences across worlds and high school grades predict college eligibility and enrollment.

Our Bridging Multiple Worlds Model focuses on how youth forge identities that coordinate their cultural and family traditions with those of their peers, schools, and communities; how relationships across worlds are both challenges and resources; and how institutions enhance or impede developmental pathways (Cooper, 1999; Cooper & Denner, 1998). In earlier research, we found that European American youth who experienced both individuality and connectedness in family communication showed greater exploration of their career identities and other domains. Conflict in the context of support, rather than support alone, was associated with adolescent development (for a review of this work, see Grotevant & Cooper, 1998). We also found evidence of continuity across family and peer worlds (Cooper & Cooper, 1992). Drawing on the Bridging Multiple Worlds model, this study examines whether African American and Latino youth who experienced both resources and challenges in their worlds would achieve higher grades and college eligibility.

The World of Outreach Programs

The university academic outreach programs that participated in this study, the Early Academic Outreach Program (EAOP) and Mathematics, Engineering, and Science Achievement (MESA), are known for their effectiveness (Edgert & Taylor, 1996). In earlier work, we observed program activities, interviewed program founders and staff, and conducted focus groups with parents and with junior high, high school, and college students in which we asked about students' *worlds, goals and values, personnel*, and *scripts* (Cooper et al., 1995; Cooper et al., 1998).

In these focus groups, students readily drew and discussed a wide array of *worlds*, including their families, countries of origin, friends' homes, churches, mosques, outreach programs, shopping malls, video arcades, school clubs, and sports. Rather than seeing their worlds as uniformly positive or negative, students perceived resources and challenges in each world. Resources were reflected in *brokering*, when parents, siblings, teachers, friends, and program staff spoke up for them in their homes, schools, or neighborhoods (Buriel, Perez, De Ment, Chavez, & Moran, 1998; Weisner et al., 1988) and provided emotional support and instrumental guidance. Students saw challenges in *gatekeeping*, when parents kept students home from school to protect them from dangers or when teachers and counselors discouraged students from taking college-prep math and science classes or tried to track them into remedial classes (Erickson & Schultz, 1993). Some students recounted struggles to maintain both academic goals and ties to friends who were not in school or were in gangs (Phelan et al., 1991). Schools and particularly neighborhoods were worlds where people expected students to fail, become pregnant, leave school, or to engage in delinquent activities. Students stated that outreach programs fostered a sense of family while providing them with skills, information, high expectations, and a sense of moral purpose to "do something good for your people" and "give back," such as by working as engineers in their communities or helping their younger siblings attend college.

This article builds on these findings to investigate—by combining strengths of qualitative and quantitative methods—how experiences of African American and Latino youth participating in outreach programs predicted their pathways to college. First, we examined students' *family backgrounds*, particularly their families' immigration history and parents' education. Kao and Tienda (1995) proposed that the academic motivation of students from newly immigrated families is fueled by the optimism, determination, and agency required for families to immigrate in the first place. Thus, we hypothesized that children of recent immigrants would be more likely to participate in outreach programs than students from second- or third-generation families. Research also indicates that African American college youth, compared to non-college youth, have more college and professional role models in their families (Coates, 1987; Duster, 1992; Taylor, 1991). Thus, we expected African American youth with college-educated parents to be more likely to participate in outreach programs. From the perspectives of these recent studies, recent family immigration and parents' college education can be both seen as social capital.

Second, we examined students' *resources and challenges* across their families, schools, peers, and community worlds. Research has shown how African American families, regardless of social class, draw on extended kin (MacAdoo, 1982), and how Latino and African American parents develop ties to community organizations, both for material support and help with children's future goals (Alva, 1991; Jarrett, 1995). Mexican American high school students in college-prep classes have reported more support and fewer difficulties than those in vocational tracks (Gibson, 1997). In another study, Chicano college students identified siblings as their primary influences, along with parents, outreach program staff, teachers, and counselors (León & McNeil, 1986). Finally, successful Chicana professionals have recalled how friendships with Anglo students helped them learn about college (Gándara & Osugi, 1994). Based on this research and the Ecocultural Students' Multiple Worlds, and Bridging Multiple Worlds models, we predicted that African American and Latino students would report both resources and challenges across their worlds and that both challenges and resources would in turn predict pathways through school.

Third, we traced students' longitudinal *pathways through math classes* required for university eligibility (Catsambis, 1994). We used math as an indicator of academic competence based on the role of math grades in admission to outreach programs and college and on the widespread concern about math as a barrier to academic success for women and ethnic minority students (America Association of University Women [AAUW], 1994). We also examined college-prep English grades and overall college-prep grade point average (GPA). In our sample, the range of math classes was restricted to college-prep courses, because the university outreach programs selected students who were likely to meet University eligibility requirements. In our earlier work, we traced longitudinal patterns of African American and Latino youth in these programs in high school math classes and grades (Cooper, Cooper et al., 1998). Some students stayed on track towards university eligibility with consistently high grades, most began on track, but slowly declined, and still others declined rapidly. As a group, the sample declined on average .21 of a grade point per semester. In this study, we traced students' math pathways across 4 years of high school as well as their subsequent college eligibility and enrollment.

Finally, we asked what factors in students' family backgrounds and in their resources and challenges across family, school, peer, and community worlds predicted their pathways to college eligibility and enrollment. A "capital" hypothesis, based on social capital models, suggests that students with more capital (such as high levels of parental education and recent immigration) would achieve at higher levels (Coleman, 1988; Cooper & Denner, 1998). A "challenge" hypothesis, based on the Bridging Multiple Worlds model, suggests that challenges can motivate students to succeed on behalf of their families and prove gatekeepers wrong, and that challenges in the context of support may foster career and college identity formation (Cooper, 1999). According to this hypothesis, students who coordinate resources with challenges would be more successful navigating personal, relational, and institutional pathways to college.

In sum, this study examined the family backgrounds of African American and Latino youth who participate in outreach programs; challenges and resources across their family, school, peer, and community worlds; longitudinal pathways through college-prep math classes; and the role of these three factors in students' later college eligibility and enrollment. We framed these questions to examine both capital and challenge models and to address issues for developmental science, youth policy, and programs that foster access to college for ethnically diverse youth.

Method

Participants

The sample was selected from a larger database to comprise equal numbers of men and women, equally divided among African American and Latino–Latina students. Wave 1 included 60 African American students (30 men, 30 women) and 60 Latino–Latina students (30 men, 30 women) in grades 6–11 ($M = 15$ years old, tenth grade), living in California. Students participated in the EAOP and MESA programs, both sponsored by the University of California.

Wave 1 data collection took place in 1994, when we recruited students attending jointly held academic enrichment activities of the programs. At Wave 1, data on student and parent ethnicities, education, and immigration were drawn from students' responses to open-ended questions on the Multiple Worlds Survey described below. Analyses of family education and immigration appear with results because of their relevance to the core questions of the study. Wave 2 included 66 of the original 120 students for whom follow-up data were available in 1999.

Academic outreach programs. The EAOP was designed to increase the numbers of underrepresented ethnic minority high school students eligible for the University of California (Hayward et al., 1997). In 1994, when our study began, it focused recruitment on African American, Latino, and Native American students; Asian students from low-income families also participated. Economic backgrounds of students varied, with substantial numbers from low-income families. It conducted summer school at UC for students (on a fee basis with scholarships available) and Saturday schools at community colleges without charge to students enrolling through their schools. Ethnic distributions of students at Saturday schools reflected areas around each community college.

MESA was designed to increase the numbers of ethnic minority students who are prepared for math-based college majors and professions. In 1994, it focused recruitment on African American, Latino, Native American, and Puerto Rican students (Smith, 1985). According to staff and published accounts (Edgert & Taylor, 1996), African American students included those from middle-income families who paid to participate because EAOP was not offered in their schools, whereas participating Latino students more often came from low-income families receiving scholarships and recruited through schools. At Wave 1, EAOP and MESA jointly sponsored summer academies, where we conducted our data collection.

Measures

The Multiple Worlds Survey was developed from focus group interviews with African American and Latino junior high, high school, and college students participating in the two programs (Cooper, Jackson, Azmitia, Lopez, & Dunbar, 1994). Some questions were adapted from Ecocultural Theory (Gallimore et al., 1993) and Students' Multiple Worlds Theory (Phelan et al., 1991). The survey asks students to describe their worlds and expectations held by people in each world. It taps challenges and resources across worlds by asking students who helps them and who causes them difficulties (*personnel*) for *instrumental scripts* (who helps you with school work; who helps you with math; who helps keep up with your responsibilities and stay organized; who helps you stay on track to college); and *emotional scripts* (who encourages you in math, who helps you feel confident; and who helps you with sexism or racism). The survey asks students to list up to three people who help or cause difficulties for each script rather than asking them to rate standardized lists of personnel. Questions about difficulties take the same form. To learn about diverse family forms, students are asked to list members of their family, where they were born, their education and job, their ethnicity or ethnicities, and the languages spoken with this person, among other questions. This open-ended response format enhances rapport with students, who routinely express appreciation for being asked about the realities of their lives rather than to respond to items based on assumed standard family structures and to "please check one box."

Academic achievement. At Wave 1, students brought copies of their report cards or transcripts and reported math and English grades. Official and self-reported grades were highly correlated for English, $r = .79$, and math, $r = .87$, and did not differ significantly in either subject. If report cards were unavailable, self-reported grades were used in analyses. Additional evidence of reliability was reflected in the correlation between student-reported grades from Wave 1 and grades in the same classes from the program database used for Wave 2 ($r = .87$).

For students in Wave 1, we assessed achievement by computing the following variables: junior high math GPA to assess competence entering high school and grades in Pre-algebra, Algebra 1, Geometry, and Algebra 2. For students remaining in Wave 2, we assessed achievement from program records of grades in math and English each semester from ninth to twelfth grade and college-prep GPA. In California, the 15 required college-prep courses are known as the "a through f" courses from their listing as (a) history or social science, 2 years; (b) English, 4 years; (c) math, 3 years, 4 recommended (covering algebra, geometry, and advanced algebra); (d) laboratory science, 2 years required, 3 recommended; (e) language other than English, 2 years required, 3 recommended; and (f) college-prep electives, 2 required.

Finally, to assess students' transition to college, we used the UC *eligibility index* computed by programs, based on college-prep GPA, SAT scores, and submitting all required materials, and we used the *college type* each student chose to attend (UC, CSU, California Community College, or other college).

Procedure

Recruiting participants began at the annual outreach program orientation, when the research staff explained the study and distributed flyers in English and Spanish. We mailed a letter, also in English and Spanish, to each family inviting them to participate. Students completed the Multiple Worlds Survey during Saturday or summer sessions, where we served pizza. Students were asked to bring copies of their report cards or transcripts and paid $5 for participating. A newsletter mailed to students' families reported preliminary findings to them.

All Wave 2 data were obtained from program records. As part of their ongoing record-keeping and formative evaluation, the programs gathered follow-up data on each graduate, with students' files including parents' education as well as students' grades, UC eligibility, college acceptance, and enrollment, indicated by students filing an official "Statement of Intent to Register." To maintain their records, programs mailed a survey to each home and made two attempts to reach the family and obtain data by telephone if families did not return the survey.

Results

The analyses were designed to help illuminate relationships among factors that might play a role in African American and Latino students' successful progress through the academic pipeline as they move through high school and into college. Three broad groups of variables were assessed: (a) *demographic variables,* to address the family backgrounds of program participants; (b) *helps and difficulties*, to address students' challenges and resources across their worlds; and (c) *academic variables*, including high school grades and college eligibility and enrollment, to map students' academic pathways to college. The analysis strategy was first to examine variables in each of these three groups to produce a descriptive picture of our sample and develop summary variables for further analyses. Then we systematically examined relationships among the three groups of variables to assess the role of family background and resources and challenges in predicting pathways to college. First we used multivariate analysis of variances (MANOVAs) to test ethnic and gender differences among each group of variables, followed by analysis of variances (ANOVAs) and tests for differences between means when appropriate. To assess other relations among variables, we used correlation, chi-square, and t tests as appropriate.

Who Participates?

The participants were self-selected by their participation in the outreach programs and for this study by ethnicity, gender, and their parents' willingness for them to participate. The 60 African American students in the sample were primarily born in the United States (97% men, all women). For parents from whom we had data, 98% of the 47 African American fathers were born in the United States, as were 87% of the 55 mothers. A very different pattern was present for the 60 Latino–Latina students: 23% of Latinas and 20% of Latinos were born outside the United States, most in Mexico. Of parents from whom we had data, 68% of the 59 mothers and 78% of the 54 fathers were born outside the United States; of these, 85% were born in Mexico.

We obtained two measures of parental education. One, gathered on the entire sample in Wave 1 as part of

the Multiple Worlds Survey, was based on students cat-
egorizing their parents' education as: less than elementary, elementary or junior high, high school, 2-year or
community college, 4-year college, or master's degree
or higher. The second measure, from Wave 2 students,
was on the survey programs sent to parents; it asked for
the highest grade each parent had completed. The two
measures were moderately correlated for mothers and
fathers, r's = .59 and .51, and showed similar patterns
of relationships to other measures throughout the analyses. Parents' education based on Wave 2 surveys
ranged from none to Ph.D. (M = 12.1 years). United
States-born parents had higher educational levels than
immigrants (M = 13.6 vs. 10.1 years); this difference
was significant for both mothers and fathers, $t(61)$ =
4.46, $p < .001$, and $t(53)$ = 2.25, $p < .03$, respectively.

Using MANOVAs on both Wave 1 and Wave 2 measures of parental education as a function of students'
gender and ethnicity consistently revealed an effect of
ethnicity, with African American parents having more
education than Latino parents. From the Wave 2 survey, African American mothers had more education
than Latino and Latinas' mothers (M = 14.63 vs. 12.18
years), $F(1, 92)$ = 21.18, $p < .001$, and African American fathers had more education than Latino fathers (M
= 13.87 vs. 11.01 years), $F(1, 92)$ = 42.22, $p < .001$,
with no gender or interaction effects. Comparing only
parents born in the United States revealed no significant ethnic group differences for fathers, but African
American mothers still had higher educational levels
than Latina mothers, $t(64)$ = 2.67, $p < .01$) based on
Wave 1 data. The effect in Wave 2 data was in the same
direction, but not significant.

Thus, the African American and Latino students in
this study, although matched for program participation
and gender distribution, differed in the educational levels of their parents and immigration experiences of
their families, with African American students more
likely to have college-educated parents born in the
United States and Latino students to have parents with
high school education or less who immigrated to the
United States.

Resources and Challenges across Students' Worlds

Students' reports of who helped and caused them
difficulties from the Multiple Worlds Survey were
compared in two ways. To create *personnel* scores, the
number of times each person was mentioned (e.g.,
peer, mother) was summed across each kind of help
and difficulty. Because there were eight kinds of help
and six kinds of difficulties, the maximum score for
each kind of personnel was 8 and 6 for help and difficulties, respectively. The mean scores for each of the
personnel categories mentioned by more than four students were as follows: mothers (3.78), fathers (2.54),

teachers (1.09), siblings (.82), self (.59), peers (.18),
and programs (.05). A repeated measures ANOVA for
amount of help across personnel was significant, $F(6,
714)$ = 86.83, $p < .001$, and a series of F-tests was used
to examine this effect. Students list mothers more than
fathers as giving them help overall ($p < .001$), and fathers more than teachers ($p < .001$). Their listing teachers, siblings, and themselves did not differ, although
each was listed more frequently than outreach programs and peers ($p < .01$). A similar repeated measures
ANOVA for difficulties was significant, $F(6, 714)$ =
13.13, $p < .001$. Students reported peers causing difficulties more than teachers (M's = .53 and .42, respectively, $p < .05$), who in turn were listed more than other
personnel (M's range from .00 to .14, all p's < .05).

To create summary scores by *script*, data were
summed across personnel within each kind of help and
difficulty (range 0–3). The mean scores for each help
script category were as follows: stay on track to college
(1.76), plan for future (1.19), meet responsibilities
(1.13), help with sexism and racism (1.09), encourage
in math (1.08), school work (1.08), help with math
(1.00), and feel special (.99). A repeated measures
ANOVA was significant, $F(7, 833)$ = 34.39, $p < .001$,
with students receiving significantly more help staying
on track to college than on other scripts.

The effects of gender and ethnicity on personnel and
scripts were examined with MANOVAs. For help from
different personnel, the only significant effect was for
gender, the result of help from peers, $F(1, 115)$ = 6.11, p
< .02, with girls reporting more help from peers than
boys. For help for different scripts, the only significant
effect was for ethnicity, accounted for by staying on
track to college, $F(1, 115)$ = 13.60, $p < .001$, with African American students reporting more help than Latino
students. For difficulties, the only significant effects
were for personnel, where a significant Ethnicity ×
Gender interaction was accounted for by difficulties
from fathers, $F(1, 116)$ = 4.97, $p < .03$; Latinas reported
more difficulties than African American women. There
was also a significant gender effect accounted for by difficulties from siblings, $F(1, 116)$ = 4.57, $p < .05$, with
women reporting more difficulties than men.

Finally, relations among measures were evaluated
with correlations. Those for help and for difficulty by
personnel are given in Table 1. Help from fathers correlated positively with help from mothers and negatively
with students' citing themselves as their source of help.
Help from peers correlated with help from teachers.
Difficulty from mothers correlated with difficulty from
fathers and siblings. The relatively small number of
significant correlations suggests that students saw help
and difficulties from different personnel quite differently, and that individual personnel scores provided
relatively independent information.

Table 2 provides similar correlations for help and
difficulties by script. For help, almost all correlations

Table 1. *Correlations among Measures of Help and Difficulty With Personnel*

	Fathers	Mothers	Siblings	Self	Peers	Teachers
Help						
Mothers	.38***					
Siblings	−.01	.12				
Self	−.24**	−.15	−.07			
Peers	−.11	−.01	−.11	.06		
Teachers	.01	.04	.02	−.10	.19*	
Programs	−.17	−.07	−.12	.14	−.06	−.04
Difficulties						
Mothers	.41***					
Siblings	.01	.26**				
Self	−.08	−.02	−.01			
Peers	−.04	−.03	.01	−.02		
Teachers	−.11	.05	.16	.11	.01	
Program	(insufficient observations)					

Note: N = 120 for all correlations.
*p < .05. **p < .01. ***p < .001.

Table 2. *Correlations Among Measures of Help and Difficulty With Scripts*

	Stay on Track to College	Encourage Math	Math	Feel Special	Plan Future	Meet Responsibilities	Racism or Sexism
Help							
Encourage Math	.20*						
Help With Math	.21*	.56***					
Feel Special	.16	.27**	.39***				
Plan Future	.23*	.34***	.40***	.42***			
Meet Responsibilities	.15	.41***	.43***	.27**	.49***		
Sexism or Racism	.11	.30***	.32***	.33***	.27**	.35**	
School Work	.15	.45***	.59***	.34***	.45***	.42***	.23*

	Discourages With Math	Difficulties With Math	Plan Future	Meet Responsibilities	Racism or Sexism
Difficulties					
Difficulties With Math	.36***				
Plan Future	.09	.06			
Meet Responsibilities	.03	.14	.22*		
Racism or Sexism	.26**	.16	.30***	.26**	
School Work	.38***	.44***	.10	.25**	.23**

Note: N = 120 for all correlations.
*p < .05. **p < .01. ***p < .001.

were significant. Although there are some plausible patterns such as help with math correlating more highly with help with school work (r = .59) than with help with sexism or racism (r = .31), t(117) = 3.11, p < .01, the overall pattern suggests that students did not differentiate the help they received on the topics surveyed. A similar pattern is shown among difficulties. In this case, over half the correlations are significant. Again, this suggests a lack of differentiation in the types of difficulties students reported. Either students experienced similar kinds of help from several people or they did not differentiate how specific people helped them.

In sum, the students reported substantially more help than difficulties, indicating more resources than

challenges for this group of students. The analyses show they saw help coming particularly from their parents and to a lesser extent from teachers, peers, and themselves, whereas difficulties came particularly from peers and teachers. For the scripts of help and difficulties (e.g., helps with math, causes difficulties with math), students appeared to make much less differentiation. Notably, both personnel and scripts for help and difficulties showed only minimal differences as a function of students' gender and ethnicity.

Students' Academic Pathways

Academic performance was assessed with four measures: grades or GPA, change in GPA over time, an index of college eligibility, and the type of college selected. Grades for any specific course were not available for all participants, and several measures, including the eligibility index, were available only for Wave 2 participants.

The overall academic performance for the sample was quite good, with GPA in college-prep courses averaging 2.95. Students' GPA in English was higher than in math (3.11 vs. 2.66), $t(59) = 5.30$, $p < .001$. Ethnic and gender effects were assessed with separate MANOVAs on Wave 1 and Wave 2 samples. For Wave 1, the dependent variables were math GPA in junior high, pre-algebra, algebra, and geometry. For Wave 2, the dependent variables were math GPA, English GPA, and college-prep GPA. No significant effects were found for either wave.

Change in performance over time was examined by looking both at whether math and English courses were taken in a given semester and at change in math and English GPA as students progressed through school. The most salient findings for this analysis of Wave 2 were that the numbers of students taking math and of students getting A's and B's declined from ninth to twelfth grade. The pattern for English was very different, with no systematic decrease in students enrolled in English or their GPA. Consistent with these patterns, students took more English than math courses, $t(65) = 2.76$, $p < .01$. The number of math courses taken correlated significantly with math GPA $r(65) = .34$, $p < .05$, but the same was not true for English. It appears that students continued in higher-level math classes only if they were succeeding. There were no gender or ethnic differences in the number of math and English courses taken.

To look at individual students' pathways through college-prep math, a slope score was computed for each student by assuming equal intervals between these courses in this order: Pre-algebra, Algebra 1A, Algebra 1B, Geometry, and Algebra 2. (The task of analyzing math pathways for Wave 1 was made complicated by different data being available for different students. If a student reported only grades for Algebra 1A and Algebra 2, which are three class intervals apart, the calculated slope would be [Algebra 2 GPA–Algebra 1A GPA)/3], not [Algebra 2 GPA–Algebra 1A GPA]/2.) The typical math pathway was one of slowly declining grades, with an average slope of −.19 of a grade point per class, which differed significantly from a 0 slope, $t(87) = 3.42$, $p < .01$. No significant ethnic or gender differences were found in this pattern.

To assess the pattern of performance through high school, slope scores were used to assess the degree to which students improved over time (positive slope), performed similarly across time (near zero slope), or performed more poorly over time (negative slope). The slope for Wave 2 data, calculated more directly by using grade in math each semester, averaged −.11, (i.e.,

an average decline of .11 GPA per semester). Again the slope was significantly less than zero, $t(65) = 2.39$, $p < .01$, with no significant gender or ethnicity effects. Each individual's slope can be used to classify them into one of four patterns. The patterns, slope criteria, and number of students exhibiting the pattern from Wave 2 are as follows: *increasers* (slope > .1), $n = 9$; *steady* (slope −.1 to +.1), $n = 20$; *slow decliners* (slope −.1 to −.2), $n = 12$; and *fast decliners* (slope < .2), $n = 17$. The underlying assumptions of a consistent linear trend in individuals' grades over time seems to characterize patterns for most students, but some students showed a rapid decline followed by recovery that we call *back on track*. Although the overall slope for these students may be close to zero, the category *steady* is not fully accurate. Examples of each of these five patterns will be presented as case studies after group-level findings.

College eligibility information, available on 49 students, was coded as follows: 3 = fully eligible ($n = 23$); 2 = students submitted all materials, but were not eligible because of at least one indicator below threshold ($n = 7$); and 1 = not all materials in and of those materials provided, at least one below threshold ($n = 19$). Two methods were used for coding the college in which each student ($n = 52$) enrolled. The first was used to create an ordinal scale reflecting the hierarchy in California higher education (3 = University of California; 2 = California State University; 1 = Community College). The second treated each of these as categorical and added a category for private or out-of-state 4-year colleges and universities. Gender and ethnicity effects were examined with a MANOVA on eligibility and college type ordinal scores. Only the ethnicity effect was significant; univariate analyses showed this resulted from college type $F(1,48) = 5.00$, $p < .05$, with African American students scoring higher than Latino students. A chi-square analysis of the four college types × ethnicity revealed equal numbers of students in each ethnic group going to UC, more Latinos and Latinas going to state universities and community colleges, and more African Americans going to private and out-of-state institutions, $\chi^2(3) = 7.83$, $p < .05$, $n = 52$. A number of historically Black colleges and universities were among this latter group, including Howard University, Morehouse College, Hampton University, and Spelman College. Thus, effects of ethnicity on the ordinal scale of college type appeared to reflect differential choices in type of institution rather than differences in prestige of institutions.

Correlations among academic performance variables are presented in Table 3. The majority showed moderate to strong correlations with other measures. College-prep GPA correlated significantly with all the others, as did English GPA and college eligibility, except with the English slope. English slope did not correlate with any other variable except math slope, but this

Table 3. *Correlations Among Academic Measures*

	Algebra	Math GPA	Math Slope	English GPA	English Slope	Eligibility	College Type
College-prep GPA	0.50*** (49)	0.75*** (58)	0.47*** (58)	0.87*** (59)	0.36** (60)	0.79*** (52)	0.44*** (58)
Algebra	1.00 (71)	0.73*** (50)	0.26 (49)	0.42** (50)	0.17 (50)	0.65*** (44)	0.21 (51)
Math GPA	0.73*** (50)	1.00 (62)	0.33** (60)	0.57*** (60)	0.08 (60)	0.68*** (51)	0.15 (54)
Math slope	0.26 (49)	0.33** (60)	1.00 (60)	0.38** (60)	0.40** (60)	0.32* (51)	0.33* (54)
English GPA	0.42** (50)	0.57*** (60)	0.38** (60)	1.00 (61)	0.24 (61)	0.73*** (52)	0.38** (58)
English slope	0.17 (50)	0.09 (60)	0.40 ** (60)	0.24 (61)	1.00 (62)	0.23 (53)	0.10 (59)
Eligibility	0.65*** (44)	0.68*** (51)	0.32* (51)	0.73*** (52)	0.23 (53)	1.00 (53)	0.30* (50)

Note: Coefficient appears with *n* of cases in parentheses.
*$p < .05$. **$p < .01$. ***$p < .001$.

correlation suggests consistent differentiation between students who were succeeding academically and those who were declining. Algebra 1 grades were correlated significantly with math GPA, English GPA, and eligibility; this course was typically taken in ninth grade and the grade not used to compute eligibility. Math slope in the first two years also correlated with math GPA, $r(28) = .37, p < .05$, and eligibility, $r(27) = .43, p < .05$, suggesting moderate predictability from early math grades to overall academic success in high school.

In sum, the overall pattern of academic pathways in our sample was one of substantial variability, but relatively high average performance. During high school, students' decreases or improvements in math and English tended to occur together in time, but changes in math were better predictors of college-prep GPA, eligibility, and college type. Finally, there was surprising predictability of these variables from students' math performance early in high school.

Do Family Background and Students' Resources and Challenges Predict Academic Pathways?

In examining interrelationships among variables, we first considered possible non-random selection of those remaining in Wave 2. A series of *t*-tests comparing those students only in Wave 1 and those in Wave 2 revealed no significant differences, either in their parents' education or on most help and difficulties variables. Wave 2 students showed a marginally significant advantage in total help, $t(118) = 1.95, p = .05$. Wave 2 students also reported more total help from teachers than the Wave 1 cohort, $t(118) = 2.89, p < .01$. No academic variables available only from Wave 1 showed even marginally significant differences between groups. Given the likelihood of some spuriously significant differences with the large number of comparisons, these results lessen our concern about selection factors in attrition, and the results of data from both waves are treated as validly characterizing students in the programs.

From the social capital perspective, we expected parents' education to be correlated with their providing

academic help and their children's academic success and progress toward college. Fathers' education did correlate with total help they provided, $r(63) = .31, p < .05$, but fathers' education also correlated negatively with students' college-prep GPA, $r(58) = -.32, p < .05$, and their eligibility, $r(51) = -.38, p < .05$. None of the correlations between mothers' education and either help and difficulties or academic measures was significant. Thus, there was little support for the social capital perspective for this sample.

The correlations among the help personnel and scripts and the academic variables are presented in Table 4 and similar correlations for difficulties in Table 5. The relatively small numbers of significant correlations lead to caution in interpreting those that are significant. It is only partially reassuring that correlations involving help are generally positive and those with difficulties, generally negative. Nevertheless, there are some interesting patterns. The correlations reported in the text are all significant at $p < .05$ (see the tables for *n*). Helping stay on track to college and encouraging in math predicted college type ($r = .24$ and $r = .30$, respectively). English GPA was correlated with total help ($r = .26$), helping feel special ($r = .26$), plan for the future ($r = .25$), and with sexism or racism ($r = .27$). For help by personnel category, fathers seemed to help with academic performance, as seen in English GPA ($r = .25$), math GPA ($r = .26$), and overall college-prep GPA ($r = .29$), whereas mothers appeared to contribute to successful transitions from high school to college, as reflected in eligibility ($r = .26$) and college type ($r = .25$). Finally, total help from siblings was related to English GPA ($r = .32$). Thus, although not powerful predictors, help, particularly from parents, did correlate with academic performance and successful transition to college.

No difficulties script was significantly correlated with academic variables. Total difficulty was negatively related only with college type ($r = -.24$). The only other significant correlations were positive, between difficulties with siblings and English GPA ($r = .32$), math GPA ($r = .36$), and math slope ($r = .27$). Thus, among students with relatively high levels of help and low levels of difficulties, differences in the amount of difficulties did not predict their academic

Table 4. *Correlations Between Help and Academic Measures*

Type of Help	College Type[a]	Eligibility[b]	College-prep GPA[c]	English GPA[d]	English Slope[e]	Math GPA[e]	Math Slope[c]
Total Help	.19	.21	.21	.26*	.16	.07	.10
Script							
Stay on Track to College	.24*	−.08	.04	−.04	.05	−.01	.16
Encourages in Math	.30*	.17	.14	.17	.04	.05	.13
Feel Special	.12	.19	.20	.26*	.10	.10	.00
Helps With Math	.05	.04	.04	.03	−.01	.03	.00
Plan Future	.20	.12	.23	.25*	.19	.08	.24
Meet Responsibilities	.11	.10	.13	.20	.23	−.01	.03
With Racism or Sexism	−.09	.20	.18	.27*	.09	.15	.02
School Work	.07	.02	.07	.09	.11	−.08	−.04
Personnel							
Fathers	.16	.24	.29*	.25*	.06	.26*	.14
Mothers	.25*	.26*	.06	.07	.11	−.09	−.05
Siblings	.15	.13	.20	.32*	.12	.05	.03
Self	.06	−.02	−.01	−.04	−.17	.07	.18
Peers	−.12	−.06	.00	.02	.11	−.19	−.07
Teachers	.00	−.21	.01	.11	.14	.05	−.02
Program	.12	−.10	.09	.03	−.01	.06	.18

[a]$n = 65$. [b]$n = 53$. [c]$n = 60$. [d]$n = 61$. [e]$n = 62$.
*$p < .05$.

Table 5. *Correlations Between Difficulties and Academic Measures*

Type of Difficulties	College Type[a]	Eligibility[b]	College-prep GPA[c]	English GPA[d]	English Slope[e]	Math GPA[e]	Math Slope[c]
Total Difficulties	−.24*	.14	−.09	−.02	−.05	.07	.11
Personnel							
Father	.02	.10	−.15	−.14	−.16	.01	.10
Mother	.00	.14	−.09	.15	−.06	.12	.20
Sibling	.01	−.08	.20	.32*	.01	.36*	.27*
Self	−.20	.17	−.23	−.23	−.17	−.12	.04
Peer	−.15	.06	−.04	−.07	.17	−.11	−.05
Teacher	−.15	.06	−.04	.08	−.15	.19	.10
Script							
Discourages With Math	−.15	.03	.09	.09	.14	.17	.06
Difficulties With Math	−.14	−.25	−.16	−.07	−.14	−.11	.08
Plan Future	−.25*	.13	−.04	.05	.11	.04	.02
Meet Responsibilities	−.06	.09	−.17	−.11	−.15	−.14	−.02
Racism or Sexism	−.05	−.07	.10	.03	−.02	.17	.05
School Work	−.24*	.11	−.13	−.05	−.08	.13	.20

[a]$n = 65$. [b]$n = 53$. [c]$n = 60$. [d]$n = 61$. [e]$n = 62$.
*$p < .05$.

outcomes, except perhaps when difficulties from siblings functioned as a challenge. These findings provide some support for the challenge hypothesis.

Mapping Students' Pathways Through School with Longitudinal Case Studies

Five prototypic pathways in math grades—steady, slowly declining, rapidly declining, increasing, and back on track—are now illustrated with longitudinal case studies. These show how group-level findings occur in individual lives and how the broad array and dis-

tinctive patterns of resources and challenges across worlds make each student's experience moving along pathways through school unique.

The most common math pathway was a *steady* one, seen in a Latina student whose parents immigrated to the United States having attended elementary school in Mexico. She saw her family world as her primary source of both help and difficulties. Her mother, father, and sister helped her across a broad range of scripts, and her older brother caused her difficulties with schoolwork and discouraged her in math. This case provides an example of a student with high math grades experiencing help from one sibling and difficulties from another. She was admitted to UC campus and enrolled there.

The *slowly declining* pathway was seen in an African American woman, a student from a two-parent household with two siblings. Both her parents had attended college. The group-level finding of parents specializing in the help they provided was seen in her mother helping her stay on track to college, keep up with responsibilities, and plan her future and her father helping with schoolwork and math. Her cousin and godmother helped her feel special, her English and science teachers helped her stay on track to college and plan her future and encouraged her in math, and her friends helped her feel special and with school work, math, and her responsibilities. She did not list any difficulties. She was admitted to a UC campus and enrolled there.

A student showing *rapidly declining* math grades was an African American student from a two-parent family whose parents had post-graduate college education. He drew resources from his family, school, peer, and community worlds. His mother helped him stay on track to college and plan the future and encouraged him in math, and his grandmother helped him feel special. His coaches helped him stay on track to college and with responsibilities, and his friends helped him with math, stay on track to college, and feel special. Yet, he also listed peers on a sports team giving him difficulty feeling confident and a friend making it hard to keep up with responsibilities. This case illustrates how students having difficulty may be receiving help, but that help does not ensure high grades. No data were available for his college admission or enrollment.

The *increasing* pathway was seen in the case of an African American student from a two-parent family with one brother and two sisters. His experiences illustrate continuity in help across worlds. Both parents had attended college. His parents, sister, and play sister helped him with his schoolwork and his parents, sister, and a teacher helped him stay on track to college. His principal, counselor, and grandparents helped him feel special. His parents and outreach program staff helped him plan the future. He saw difficulties coming from peers at school in schoolwork and racism in the broader society. He was admitted to UC, but chose to enroll in a private out-of-state university.

Finally, the *back on track* pathway was seen in the case of a Latino, a student from a two-parent family. His parents were born in Mexico, his mother a high school graduate and his father completing three years of elementary school. All his resources were from his family world, and he primarily experienced challenges in his family and peer worlds. Both parents encouraged him in math and helped him stay on track to college and with sexism and racism. He listed his older brother as a resource for all forms of help. His difficulties came from his father with schoolwork and his peers with sexism and racism. This case shows how an older sibling

can play a key role in helping a student navigate across family, school, and peer worlds. The student was accepted and enrolled at a UC campus.

Discussion

We first summarize the most salient findings with respect to the four questions that organized the study and then examine them with respect to current scholarly debates. We conclude by discussing the implications of this work in the broader context of integrating research, policy, and practice for the academic pipeline problem facing ethnically diverse youth.

Amid their resources and challenges—personal, relational, institutional, and cultural, a remarkable number of students in this study were successful in completing high school and gaining admission to colleges and universities. The African American participants more typically had U. S. born, college-educated parents and Latino students, immigrant parents with a high school education or less. As a group, students reported substantial help from a variety of sources, particularly their parents and teachers. Compared to their resources, students reported fewer difficulties, primarily from their peers and teachers. Students' academic performance showed substantial stability, although math grades tended to drift downward. Early math grades predicted overall academic performance, and changes in math and English tended to occur together, with decreases in math particularly linked to poorer academic outcomes. Despite the range of parental education and immigration histories, these family background variables played only a modest role in predicting students' academic performance. Surprisingly, fathers' educational level was negatively related to college-prep GPA and college eligibility. Although mothers' and fathers' help correlated positively with more than one academic outcome, as did siblings causing difficulty, overall levels of help and difficulties were not strong predictors of academic performance.

Who are the Students?

The demographic profiles of students participating in the outreach programs revealed very different patterns for African Americans and Latinos. The African American students in the sample, all but one born in the United States, were likely to have college-educated parents also born in the United States. The Latino students, more than 20% of whom were born outside the United States, were likely to have immigrant parents with a high school education or less. Thus, African American youth in the sample were more likely to be following their parents' pathways to college and Latino youth, beginning to exceed their parents' education. These demographic profiles raise questions of self-selection and representativeness of the sample that bear upon generalizing from the findings. Because the communities from which students came to the programs include a broader range of social class than that represented in our sample, a key question for research and practice concerns why more low-income African American youth and second- and third-generation Latino youth were not participating in outreach programs. One possibility is that the Saturday and summer academies of the outreach programs conflicted with students' work schedules; another is that for relatively recent immigrants, time in the United States is associated with growing alienation from schools (Fordham & Ogbu, 1986). A third is that the information distribution and recruiting of outreach programs does not reach all families equally.

Resources and Challenges Across Students' Worlds

Students reported relatively high levels of help and low levels of difficulties, with few differences as a function of ethnicity. Students from both ethnic groups appeared to be getting high levels of help from adults, especially parents and teachers, and experiencing difficulties primarily from peers and teachers. This pattern is inconsistent with the common negative stereotypes of ethnic minority parents and the teachers of their children. Resources and challenges often emerged from the same individuals and the same world. Correlations among measures of helps and difficulties suggest students had a differentiated picture of who helped or caused them difficulty. They also suggest coherence in students' experiences in the family, with 4 of 5 significant correlations involving father, mother, sibling, and self. Although peers and teachers are often seen as occupying different worlds, students' interactions with peers and teachers often occur at school, so the significant correlation between help for teachers and peers might indicate coherence of experience in a single world.

Examining help and difficulties as a function of scripts provided much less differentiation. All measures of help except staying on track to college correlated significantly with every other measure of help, and over half of the correlations among difficulties were significant. It might be that although only some personnel offered help or cause difficulties, they did so across a broad range of scripts. Or it might be that students remember who helps them or causes them difficulty, but attend less to its form. By interviewing parents and teachers about students' resources and challenges could differentiate these two explanations and provide converging evidence for students' views.

The unexpected finding from the open-ended format, that allowed students to name anyone as helping or causing difficulties, was that students named themselves as doing both. Future research could probe this

finding as well as compare students' views of themselves with those of parents, teachers, and peers.

Finally, the minimal ethnic and gender effects suggest that for students in outreach programs, the range of challenges and difficulties they encounter are comparable despite differences in their family backgrounds. The finding that all groups in outreach programs received relatively high and comparable levels of help and relatively low and comparable levels of difficulties should interest program staff and parents. However, it raises the question of whether these experiences are specific to students in these programs or generally characterize students in schools from which participants are drawn. A more inclusive school-based sample is required to answer this question.

Math Pathways

Examining students' math pathways and broader academic pathways revealed a picture of an academically strong sample. Overall, students in the outreach programs maintained about a 2.6 college-prep math GPA and 3.0 overall college-prep GPA. Measures of academic performance were highly correlated, except for English slope and type of college selected. Math and English slopes were correlated, suggesting that students' high school grades form coherent pathways rather than reflecting only performance in particular subjects or with particular teachers. These trends highlight the plausibility of studying effects of resources and challenges from a variety of worlds to understand students' academic pathways.

The few significant correlations with college type (college-prep GPA, math slope, and English GPA) indicate that when students select what college to attend, they consider factors other than the prestige of colleges accepting them. Categorical analyses showing more Latino students choosing California State Universities and community colleges and more African American students choosing private or out-of-state colleges and universities provide further evidence for this point. Community colleges are the least expensive option and may appeal to students with limited financial resources even if they qualify for more prestigious institutions. Historically Black colleges and universities may have appealed to some African American students and their families, particularly as the politics of affirmative action became heated in California. These results highlight the importance of gathering information on where students are accepted, where they choose to attend, and how students' relationships across worlds affect their decisions.

The high level of intercorrelations among the other academic measures warrants several comments. First, math and English GPA are not independent of college-prep GPA, so the correlation of each with college-prep GPA is expected. In addition, because more English than math class grades go into calculating college-prep GPA for most students, the higher correlation between overall grades with English than math is not surprising. The two slope scores are mathematically independent of college-prep GPA except for ceiling and floor effects, so the significant correlation with math slope is interesting. It suggests that viewing math as a key constraint on pathways to college is appropriate. In addition, the significant correlation of college-prep GPA with Algebra 1 (usually taken in ninth grade and thus mathematically independent), suggests that attending to math grades early would help guide students towards college eligibility.

A key finding distinguishing this study of outreach program participants was the lack of ethnicity or gender effects on math GPA, math slope, or number of math courses taken. Despite the very good overall performance of men and women in both ethnic groups, the correlation between math courses taken with math GPA suggests these findings cannot be attributed to ceiling effects. The lack of gender effects is an exception to the commonly reported pattern of women scoring more poorly than men (AAUW, 1994). Furthermore, the overall high level of academic achievement of this sample of African American and Latino youth also contrasts with the frequently reported poorer performance of these groups relative to Anglo or Asian American groups (Catsambis, 1994; Davenport et al., 1998).

Predicting Pathways to College

In predicting school pathways from parental demographics and students' resources and challenges, the first issue is the relatively low predictability found in this study. Other research shows correlations between parents' education and children's academic success. Why might we have found no links for mothers' education and negative correlations for fathers' education with college-prep GPA and eligibility? One possibility is that parents' education is related to activities like getting children into programs such as those in this study (Useem, 1992). Focusing only on students in such programs may have prevented our detecting the impact of parental education. Similarly, correlations of helps and difficulties with academic measures may be attenuated because students who are supported to attend and remain in programs may also experience high levels of help and low levels of difficulties and be more academically successful. Thus, the modest predictability in this study might be taken more seriously than if it had been found in a broader sample.

Although the number and size of significant correlations of help and difficulties with academic measures was smaller than expected, interesting patterns still emerged. Mothers' and fathers' help were strongly correlated with each other, but differentially related to academic variables, with fathers' help predicting academic performance (math, English, and overall college-prep GPA) and mothers' help predicting outcomes requiring organization and decision-making as well as academic performance (eligibility and college type). For example, eligibility is dependent on college-prep GPA, but also requires signing up for standardized tests and submitting essays and letters that may compensate for lower test scores or GPA. Similarly, college type is influenced by considerations beyond eligibility. The possibility that parents play complementary roles in guiding their children towards college merits further study.

Such complementarity patterns may also be seen in the negative correlations between difficulties from siblings and students' performance in math and English. These might be interpreted as supporting the challenge hypothesis, in which students may work to excel in response to siblings' criticism. Also relevant to the challenge hypothesis was our finding many students naming siblings as resources as well as challenges. Alternatively, siblings may be ambivalent about students' achievement and react by causing difficulties; in this case, students' achievement might elicit difficulties rather than difficulties fostering achievement. Another possibility is that siblings' challenges may spark students' awareness that not everyone values academic success; this metacognitive development may foster students' ability to identify challenges and address them. Further research on students' efficacy, such as in language brokering, will illuminate the paradoxical costs and benefits of resources and challenges (e.g., Buriel et al., 1998).

This study was not ideally designed to test hypotheses about the role of parental education or generation of immigration in college eligibility. These variables were not controlled and were confounded with and covaried with ethnicity, a variable that was part of the design. Nevertheless, the lack of correlation of immigration history and the paradoxical negative correlations of fathers' education with student achievement contrast with other reports of immigrant students performing better than second-generation youth and of higher parental education predicting school success (Gibson, 1997). Our sample included students whose parents grew up in and out of the United States and had high and low levels of schooling, yet in each group we found students succeeding. Thus, variables like immigration status and low educational level of parents do not reflect obstacles students cannot overcome. Although these demographic variables will continue to play a part in research and policy, identifying causal mechanisms is crucial for building strategies that policy makers, practitioners, families, and students themselves can use.

Integrating Research, Policy, and Practice on the Pipeline Problem

Most analyses of the academic pipeline problem focus either on African American students and Black–White comparisons (Bowen & Bok, 1998; Duster, 1992) or on Latino students (Latino Eligibility Task Force, 1993). For California and Texas, where Latino youth are projected to become the majority in public schools and in other states with growing Latino populations, mapping similarities and differences between African American and Latino students is timely. Our findings for both Latino and African American youth indicate the importance of resources from families, schools, peers, and programs (rather than only parents' education), of students' social and personal challenges, and of their own actions in succeeding in the increasingly difficult college-prep courses that lead to university eligibility.

At the time of data collection, the demographic background of students participating in each program reflected the California legal mandate to increase the numbers of underrepresented ethnic minority students attending the UC, as well as distinctive mandates for each program (Edgert & Taylor, 1996). For example, MESA recruited students to enhance the ethnic diversity of mathematics and science professions without regard for socioeconomic background. Although affirmative action in university admissions based on ethnicity and gender has ended in California, debate continues on how to achieve a diverse student body through alternative criteria, including family income, parental education, and geography (urban, rural, or suburban *residence*). Meanwhile, interest grows in monitoring demographic characteristics of students who do and do not participate in outreach programs and their motivation for doing so. For example, in 1998, the California Legislative Analysts' Office asked the University:

> to compare ... K–12 performance, high school graduation rate, college performance, college graduation rate, and employment experience of participants in each outreach program, with comparable groups of nonparticipants ... The study design should...be based on statistical techniques that control for personal and socioeconomic differences among participants and non-participants ... (and) evaluate the extent to which selection criteria of programs and participation decisions of students affect outcomes. (1998, p. 1)

Challenges generalizing from studies of outreach program were addressed by Gándara et al. (1998), who compared participants in three prominent programs by scores on standardized eighth-grade achievement tests. Whereas the high school Puente Project drew students from the upper three quartiles, the Achievement Via Individual Determination (AVID) program drew from the 50th to 75th percentile to avoid "creaming" or targeting top students whose success might be seen as occurring without the program, and the Achievement for Latinos through Academic Success (ALAS) program drew from the lowest quartile. Collaborations across such competitive, selective, and inclusive programs are bringing universities and schools into mutually satisfy-

ing partnerships (Haycock, 1996). Researchers and program evaluators paying careful attention to participating students, including their academic skills, will improve our understanding of the realities of their lives and what programs should provide for the diverse students in U.S. schools.

Longitudinal case studies may be particularly useful in understanding these realities. This study yielded longitudinal case studies illustrating five prototypic pathways—steady, slowly declining, rapidly declining, increasing, and "back on track." These cases illuminate how group-level findings occur in individual lives and how distinctive resources and challenges across worlds made each student's pathway through school unique. Longitudinal case studies are useful for examining how elements of a theoretical model are configured in individual lives rather than only examining disaggregated concepts and variables. For this reason, such cases are meaningful for researchers, policy analysis, practitioners, and community members, including youth and families.

Finally, through outreach programs, school-based partnerships, and school-to-work programs in the United States and other nations, youth can become part of larger networks of community resources (Chisholm, Büchner, Krüger, & Brown, 1990). We need to understand how students enter and persist in college and work as they develop competence across their multiple worlds. Asking who participates, what are indicators of pathways on common metrics, and what program components engage students with different needs can benefit multiple stakeholders. Although we note their limitations in presenting results of this study, we believe research methods that gather data from more than one world of youth and link quantitative and qualitative analyses offer productive tools for such partnerships.

References

Alva, S. A. (1991). Academic invulnerability among Mexican–American students: The importance of protective resources and appraisals. *Hispanic Journal of Behavioral Sciences, 13*, 18–34.

America Association of University Women. (1995). *How schools shortchange girls - The AAUW Report: A study of major findings on girls and education*. New York: Marlowe.

Bowen, W. G., & Bok, D. (1998). *The shape of the river: Long-term consequences of considering race in college and university admissions*. Princeton, NJ: Princeton University Press.

Buriel, R., Perez, W., De Ment, T. L., Chavez, D. V., & Moran, V. R. (1998). The relationship of language brokering to academic performance, biculturalism, and self-efficacy among Latino adolescents. *Hispanic Journal of Behavioral Sciences, 20*, 283–297.

Catsambis, S. (1994). The path to math: Gender and racial-ethnic differences in mathematics participation from middle school to high school. *Sociology of Education, 67*, 199–215.

Chisholm, L., Büchner, P., Krüger, H-H., & Brown, P. (1990). *Childhood, youth, and social change: A comparative perspective*. London: Falmer Press.

Coates, D. L. (1987). Gender differences in the structure and support characteristics of black adolescents' social networks. *Sex Roles, 17,* 667–687.

Coleman, J. S. (1988). Social capital in the creation of human capital. *American Journal of Sociology Supplement, 94,* 95–120.

Cooper, C. R. (1999). Cultural perspectives on individuality and connectedness in adolescent development. In A. Masten (Ed.), *Minnesota symposia on child psychology: Culture and development.* (pp. 25–57). Hillsdale, NJ: Lawrence Erlbaum Associates, Inc.

Cooper, C. R., & Cooper, R. G. (1992). Links between adolescents' relationships with their parents and peers: Models, evidence, and mechanisms. In R. D. Parke & G. W. Ladd (Eds.) *Family-peer relationships: Modes of linkages* (pp. 135–158). Hillsdale, NJ: Lawrence Erlbaum Associates, Inc.

Cooper, C. R. et al. (1998). Mathematical models of capital and challenges in the college identities of African American and Latino youth. Paper presented at the meetings of the International Society for the Study of Behavioral Development, Berne, Switzerland.

Cooper, C. R., & Denner, J. (1998). Theories linking culture and psychology: Universal and community-specific processes. *Annual Review of Psychology, 49,* 559–584.

Cooper, C. R., Jackson, J. F., Azmitia, M., & Lopez, E. M. (1998). Multiple selves, multiple worlds: Ethnically sensitive research on identity, relationships, and opportunity structures in adolescence. In V. McLoyd & L. Steinberg (Eds.), *Conceptual and methodological issues in the study of minority adolescents and their families.* (pp. 111–126). Hillsdale, NJ: Lawrence Erlbaum Associates, Inc.

Cooper, C. R., Jackson, J. F., Azmitia, M., Lopez, E. M., & Dunbar, N. (1994). *Multiple worlds survey: Qualitative and quantitative versions.* University of California, Santa Cruz.

Cooper, C. R., Jackson, J. F., Azmitia, M., Lopez, E. M., & Dunbar, N. (1995). Bridging students' multiple worlds: African American and Latino youth in academic outreach programs. In R. F. Macías & R. G. García Ramos (Eds.), *Changing schools for changing students: An anthology of research on language minorities* (pp. 211–234). Santa Barbara, CA: University of California Linguistic Minority Research Institute.

Davenport, E. C., Davison, M. L., Kuang, H., Ding, S., Kim, S., & Kwak, N. (1998). High school mathematics course-taking by gender and ethnicity. *American Educational Research Journal, 35,* 497–514.

Duster, T. S. (1992). *Making the future different: Report of the Task Force on Black Student Eligibility.* Berkeley, CA: University of California.

Edgert, P., & Taylor, J. W. (1996). *Progress report on the effectiveness of collaborative student academic development programs.* (Report No. 96–11). Sacramento, CA: California Postsecondary Education Commission.

Erickson, F., & Schultz, J. (1982). *The counselor as gatekeeper: Social interaction in interviews.* New York: Academic Press.

Fordham, S., & Ogbu, J. U. (1986). Black students' school success: Coping with the "burden of 'acting white.'" *The Urban Review, 18,* 176–206.

Gallimore, R., Goldenberg, C. N., & Weisner, T. S. (1993). The social construction and subjective reality of activity settings: Implications for community psychology. *American Journal of Community Psychology, 21,* 537–559.

Gándara, P. (1995). *Over the ivy walls: The educational mobility of low-income Chicanos.* New York: State University of New York Press.

Gándara, P., Larson, K., Mehan, H., & Rumberger, R. (1998). *Capturing Latino students in the academic pipeline* (Project Rep. No. 1). Sacramento, CA: Chicano/Latino Policy Project. (ERIC Document Reproduction Service No. ED427094).

Gándara, P., & Osugi, L. (1994). Educationally ambitious Chicanas. *The NEA Higher Education Journal, 10,* 7–35.

Geiser, S. (1996). California's changing demographics: Implications for UC. In S. Golub (Ed.), *Academic outreach and intersegmental partnerships: Outreach forum proceedings* (pp. 12–14). Irvine, CA: Center for Educational Partnerships.

Gibson, M. (1997). Complicating the immigrant/involuntary minority typology. *Anthropology and Education Quarterly, 28,* 431–454.

Grotevant, H. D., & Cooper, C. R. (1998). Individuality and connectedness in adolescent development: Review and prospects for research on identity, relationships, and context. In E. Skoe & A. von der Lippe (Eds.), *Personality development in adolescence: A cross national and life span perspective.* (pp. 3–37). London: Routledge.

Haycock, K. (1996). Thinking differently about school reform. *Change, 28,* 13–18.

Hayward, G. C., Brandes, B. G., Kirst, M. W., & Mazzeo, C. (1997). *Higher education outreach programs: A synthesis of evaluations.* Berkeley, CA: Policy Analysis for California Education.

Jarrett, R. L. (1995). Growing up poor: The family experience of socially mobile youth in low-income African American neighborhoods. *Journal of Adolescent Research, 10,* 111–135.

Kao, G. & Tienda, M. (1995). Optimism and achievement: The educational performance of immigrant youth. *Social Science Quarterly, 76,* 1–19.

Latino Eligibility Task Force. (1993). *Latino student eligibility and participation in the University of California* (Rep. no. 1). University of California, Santa Cruz, CA.

Legislative Analysts' Office (1998). *Supplemental Report Language University of California Item 6440-001-0001: Cost effectiveness of student outreach programs.* Sacramento, CA: California State Legislature.

León, D. H., & McNeil, D. (1986). Chicano college students: Personal influence on decisions to enroll. *Journal of College Student Personnel, 27,* 562–564.

MacAdoo, H. P. (1982). Stress absorbing systems in Black families. *Family Relations, 31,* 479–488.

Phelan, P., Davidson, A. L., & Yu, H. C. (1991). Students' multiple worlds: Navigating the borders of family, peer, and school cultures. In P. Phelan & A. L. Davidson (Eds.), *Cultural diversity: Implications for education* (pp. 52–88). New York: Teachers College Press.

Reese, L., Gallimore, R., Goldenberg, C., & Balzano, C. (1995). Immigrant Latino parents' future orientations for their children. In R. F. Macías & R. G. G. Ramos (Eds.), *Changing schools for changing students: An anthology of research on language minorities* (pp. 205–230). Santa Barbara, CA: University of California Linguistic Minority Research Institute.

Rogoff, B. (1990). *Apprenticeship in thinking: Cognitive development in social context.* New York: Oxford University Press.

Smith, M. P. (1985). Early identification and support: The University of California-Berkeley's MESA Program. *College-School Collaboration: Appraising the Major Approaches. New Directions for Teaching and Learning, 24,* 19–25.

Taylor, R. L. (1991). Black youth, role models and the social construction of identity. In R. L. Jones (Ed.), *Black adolescents.* (pp. 155–174). Berkeley, CA: Cobb & Henry.

Useem, E. L. (1992). Middle schools and math groups: Parents' involvement in children's placement. *Sociology of Education, 65,* 263–279.

Weisner, T. S., Gallimore, R., & Jordan, C. (1988). Unpackaging cultural effects on classroom learning: Native Hawaiian peer assistance and child-generated activity. *Anthropology and Education Quarterly, 19,* 327–351.

Received March 26, 1999
Final revision received September 20, 1999
Accepted May 4, 2000

Applied Developmental Science
2002, Vol. 6, No. 2, 88–94

Family Environment and Achievement Among Three Generations of Mexican American High School Students

James L. Rodríguez
San Diego State University

This study examined generational differences in the perceptions of family environment and achievement of 3,681 Mexican American high school students. There were four family environment variables: family involvement, family monitoring, family control, and familism. Analysis of covariance procedure revealed first and second generation students reported significantly higher grades and higher levels of family monitoring than third generation students, while third generation students reported significantly higher levels of family involvement. Regression analyses revealed that family involvement was a significant predictor of student grades across all three generations of students. Results are discussed in terms of increasing our understanding the achievement of Mexican American adolescents and the role of their families in the educational process. Implications for the development and implementation of policy, prevention, and intervention programs for Mexican American adolescents and their families are discussed.

Over the past decade, interest in parent involvement programs and school-community partnerships has been increasing steadily (e.g., Epstein, 1996). It is thought that parent involvement in education and the development of school-community partnerships contribute to the academic achievement and psychological development of children and adolescents (e.g., Eccles & Harold, 1996; Epstein, 1996). However, researchers have only recently begun to explore ways to bridge the cultural discontinuities, which can exist between the home and school experiences of Mexican American children and adolescents (Delgado-Gaitan, 1991; Delgado-Gaitan, 1994; Valdes, 1996). The cultural discontinuities between the home and school experiences of Mexican American students can be magnified by language differences which impede communication between parents, students, and teachers. Furthermore, immigrant parents themselves may have limited educational experiences and may be unfamiliar with the education system in the United States (Suarez-Orozco & Suarez-Orozco, 1995; Valdes, 1996).

In addition intergenerational conflict between children and adults in immigrant families may result from differences in their respective schooling experiences. However, researchers have recently noted that children can serve as cultural and linguistic interpret-

ers for their parents (Buriel & De Ment, 1997; Garcia Coll & Magnuson, 1997). As children progress through the schooling process they acquire linguistic and socialization skills at a faster rate than their parents. Essentially, children's schooling experiences accelerates their rate of acculturation. An outcome of their accelerated acculturation is that children and adolescents from immigrant families may assume roles of responsibility within the family pertaining to interactions with schools and other institutions such as banks, utilities, and the judicial system. These roles may include a range of activities ranging from serving as interpreters for parents to providing parents with basic information concerning financial, legal, and educational matters.

The notion of children and adolescents acting as cultural brokers for their parents and other adult family members exemplifies efforts to understand the relationship of the home environment to public institutions including schools. Research on cultural brokering parallels studies that have explored the relationship between family support factors and the academic performance of Mexican American adolescents (Hernandez, 1993; Suarez-Orozco & Suarez-Orozco, 1995; Valdes, 1996).

In a study of non-immigrant Mexican descent adolescents Hernandez (1993) found family support to be a key predictor of academic resiliency. However, generational analyses were not possible in this study since the subject population did not include immigrant generation adolescents. Suarez-Orozco and Suarez-Orozco (1995) were able to address this issue in a study in which they found that family support was greater for adoles-

The research reported in this article was a portion the author's doctoral dissertation and was presented at the Society for Research in Child Development Biennial Meeting, Albuquerque, NM, March 1999.

Requests for reprints should be sent to James L. Rodríguez, College of Education, San Diego State University, 5500 Campanile Drive, San Diego, CA 92182–1153. E-mail: jlrodrig@mail.sdsu.edu

cents from immigrant Mexican families who also attained higher achievement levels than their adolescent counterparts from non-immigrant descent families. Finally, in her ethnography of 10 Mexican descent families, Valdes (1996) points out the need to study and understand culturally-driven variations in Mexican American family support systems for children's education which may differ significantly from Euroamerican family support systems. Valdes cautions that intervention efforts such as parenting programs may cause more long-term harm to immigrant families than any short-term benefits.

Although these studies indicate a relation between family support factors and academic achievement, questions concerning the role of generation status within this relation remain unanswered. It is important to understand how the family environment impacts achievement in similar and dissimilar ways for immigrant and non-immigrant adolescents. This is especially critical for Mexican American adolescents who may experience a cultural discontinuity between the home and school environments. They may be adapting to and within a school environment, which is incongruent with their home environment leading the adolescent to function between the two environments instead of within them.

This study examines the relationship between the family environment and achievement of Mexican American high school students. Four family environment variables are studies: family involvement in education, family monitoring of adolescent extracurricular activities, family control of adolescent activities, and familism, which measures the extent of familial affiliation. The family involvement variable is not limited to parent involvement in school activities. Instead it is extended to other family members (i.e. older siblings) who may also play a critical role in the adolescent's education. Family control and monitoring are limited to the role of parents within the family environment. More specific, this study examines the how adolescents' perception of the family environment may differ given their generational status.

Method

Data Collection

A 346-item questionnaire was distributed to students at three California high schools. The questionnaire included several scales and sub-scales, which measured various psychological, cultural, and educational constructs. The questionnaire, which was available in an English and Spanish version, was administered within classrooms and students were instructed to take their time in completing the questionnaire. Of the 7,140 questionnaires that were completed, 3,681 were completed by Mexican American students. A total of 441 Spanish version questionnaires were completed; the majority by Mexican American students.

Participants

The 3,681 students who identified themselves as Mexican, Mexican American, or Chicano were included in the study. There were 1,403 students identified as first generation. These students were born in Mexico and had immigrated to the United States as children. There were 1,237, second generation students who were born in the United States, but had at least one parent who was born in Mexico. There were 1,017 third generation students who were born in the United States, as were both of their parents. An important note is that there were generational differences in the reported levels of parents' educational attainment. The mean number of years of schooling for first and second generation parents was 8.6 and 9.1 years respectively, whereas it was 11.8 years for third generation parents.[1]

In addition, among the Mexican Americans there were 1,833 women and 1,837 men students. There were 11 Mexican American students who did not report their gender. Students were enrolled in student grades 9–12 and there were diminishing numbers of students in each grade from 1,020 ninth-grade students to 731 twelfth-grade students.

Measures

Four variables that measured student perceptions of the family environment were used in the study. These variables were constructed using a principal components procedure and tested for their reliability. In addition, student self-reports of grades were used as a measure of academic achievement in the study. Finally, several demographic variables were included in the study.

Family environment variables. The items used to construct each of the family variables in the study were entered into a factor analysis using a principal components method with a varimax rotation. Items were included in a factor if they had a factor loading which approached .50 or greater for a single factor. Altogether, there were four family factors were identified. In addition, the reliability of the variables in the study was assessed using Cronbach's Alpha estimate of internal consistency.

A total of 18 likert items were used to construct four family environment variables (see Table 1). All items

---

[1]Parents educational attainment was determined by taking the average of both parents level of education, except when there was a single parent household.

Table 1. *Items Used to Create Family Environment Variables*

Family Monitoring
  How much do your parents really know...
    1. Who your friends are?
    2. Where you go at night?
    3. How you spend your money?
    4. What you do with your free time?
    5. Where you are most afternoons after school?

Family Control
  Who makes most of the decisions on each of these topics?
    6. How late at night I can stay out.
    7. Which friends to go out with.
    8. Whether I get a part-time job.
    9. At what age I can leave school.
    10. How I spend my money.
    11. When I can start dating.

Family Involvmement
  How often do the people in your family:
    12. Go to school programs for parents (Open school night)?
    13. Watch you in sports or activities?
    14. Help you in choosing your courses?
    15. Go to conferences with your teachers–counselors?

Familism
    16. I should try to keep in touch with my relatives but sometimes it is better not to see them very often.
    17. It is best not to see relatives too often because they create problems for me.
    18. Friends are more dependable in times of need than relatives.

Table 2. *Rotated Factor Loadings for Family Variables*

Item	Monitoring[a]	Control[b]	Involvement[c]	Familism[d]
1	**.54**	−.06	.27	.04
2	**.70**	.25	.05	−.01
3	**.71**	.17	.09	.05
4	**.78**	.13	.09	.02
5	**.73**	.12	.06	.03
6	.16	**.59**	−.01	−.03
7	.17	**.65**	.01	.01
8	.03	**.62**	.16	−.01
9	−.06	**.47**	.14	.09
10	.12	**.56**	.06	.07
11	.18	**.65**	−.05	−.10
12	.14	.07	**.71**	.02
13	.09	−.04	**.70**	.07
14	.13	.20	**.66**	.06
15	.07	.09	**.74**	-.05
16	−.03	.01	.01	**.75**
17	.06	.01	.02	**.78**
18	.07	.04	.04	**.61**
Eigenvalue	3.75	1.83	1.55	1.49
% Variance	20.80	10.20	8.60	8.30

[a]α = .77. [b]α = .64. [c]α = .77. [d]α = .54.

were adjusted to a 5-point scale. Family involvement measured the level of family members' involvement in school-related activities. Family involvement was determined by asking students about family participation in school-related events and activities such as teacher conferences. Four items were used to construct family involvement, which had an alpha reliability coefficient of .70. *Family monitoring* measured the extent to that parents are aware of the extra-curricular and social activities of students such as where they spend time after school. Five items were used to construct family monitoring which had an alpha reliability coefficient of .77. Family *control* measured the nature of decision making within the family environment. It measured the extent to which restrictions were placed upon adolescent social activities and peer relationship such as having a girlfriend or boyfriend. Family control had an alpha reliability coefficient of .64. *Familism* measured adolescents' perceived worth of spending time with their families. Three items were used to construct familism, which had an alpha reliability coefficient of .54. The factor loadings, alpha coefficients, and eigenvalues for the four family environment variables can be seen in Table 2.

Demographic and educational variables. Generation status, and parents' education were included as variables in the study. Three levels of generation status

(first, second, and third) were determined through student's and parent's place of birth. Parents' education was determined by taking the mean number of years of parents' schooling. In single parent households, the single parent's years of schooling was used.

Finally, students' self-reported student grades were used as a measure of student achievement. Essentially, self-reported grades were used as a proxy for grade point average. In previous studies, researchers using a similar questionnaire found that teacher assigned student grades correlated highly, .76, with adolescents' self-reported student grades (Dornbusch, Ritter, Mont-Reynaud, & Chen, 1990; Dornbusch, Ritter, Leiderman, Roberts, & Fraleigh, 1987). Students were asked, "Which of the following best describes your student grades so far in high school?" Responses to this item ranged from 1 "Mostly below D's" to 8 "Mostly A's." Grades were adjusted to a 4-point scale.

Results

Analyses of Variance with a Covariate

Using generation as an independent variable Analysis of Covariance (ANCOVA) procedures were conducted for each of the family environment variables as well as for student grades. Parents' level education was entered as a covariate. Scheffé's multiple comparison tests were conducted for variables, in which there was a main effect.

Covariate effects. There were significant covariate effects (parents' level of education) for family

Table 3. *Adjusted Means, Standard Deviations, and F values Based on Analysis of Covariance (ANCOVA) by First, Second, and Third Generation Students*

	1st Generation		2nd Generation		3rd Generation		
	M	*SD*	*M*	*SD*	*M*	*SD*	**F-Value**
Family							
Involvement	2.49 a	0.51	2.55 b	0.51	2.63 ab	0.56	4.65*
Monitoring	3.82 a	0.48	3.74 b	0.49	3.62 ab	0.49	10.80**
Control	2.42	0.72	2.45	0.68	2.39	0.69	0.11
Familism	2.38	0.58	2.31	0.57	2.36	0.59	0.26
Outcome							
Grades	2.63 a	1.48	2.58 b	1.51	2.48 ab	1.62	9.26**

*$p < .05$. **$p < .001$.

involvement, $F(1, 3542) = 257.89$, $p < .001$, family monitoring, $F(1, 3559) = 16.02$, $p < .001$, and familism, $F(1, 3539) = 3.90$, $p < .05$. Since covariate effects were found for three of the five dependent variables, adjusted means were reported and Scheffé's multiple comparison tests were conducted. Scheffé's test is widely accepted for making post hoc comparisons is considered appropriate to use when there are covariate effects (Shavelson, 1996).

Generation main effects.

There were generation main effects for family involvement and family monitoring. There was a significant main effect for family involvement, $F(2, 3542) = 4.65, p < .05$, and for family monitoring $F(2, 3559) = 10.80, p < .001$). Multiple comparison tests showed that third generation students reported more family involvement ($M = 2.63$) than first and second generation students ($M = 2.49$ and 2.55) respectively. Multiple comparison tests for family monitoring showed that first and second generation students ($M = 3.82$ and 3.74) reported more family monitoring than third generation students ($M = 2.33$). There was also a main effect for grades $F(2, 3534) = 9.26$, $p < .001$. Multiple comparison tests using Scheffé's method showed that while first generation students reported the highest grades ($M = 2.63$) which differed significantly from third generation students ($M = 2.48$), they did not significantly differ from the grades of second generation students ($M = 2.58$). Table 3 displays the adjustment means, standard deviations, and F values for the generation effects.

Stepwise Regression Analyses

Four stepwise regression procedures were conducted with student grades as the dependent variable for each generation of students as well as for the entire group of subjects. The four family support variables were entered as independent variables. A summary of the results of the four stepwise regression procedures is displayed in Table 4.

Three generation model. The stepwise regression procedure for the entire sample of students yielded two significant predictors of grades. Family involvement, $F(1, 3571) = 116.99, p < .0001$, and family monitoring $F(2, 3570) = 51.64, p < .0001$) were positive predictors of grades for the entire sample of Mexican American high school students. Higher levels of family involvement and family monitoring predicted

Table 4. *Stepwise Regression Analyses With Grades as the Dependent Variable*

Variable	β	Change in r	Included in F
All Students[a]			
Involvement	0.128	0.031	116.99***
Monitoring	0.096	0.014	51.64***
Control	0.023		
Familism	0.002		
Total variance in student grades explained by the independent variables is 4.5%.			
First Generation Students[b]			
Involvement	0.136	0.035	49.49***
Monitoring	0.063	0.006	29.19***
Control	−0.003		
Familism	−0.037		
Total variance in student grades explained by the independent variables Is 4.1%.			
Second Generation Students[c]			
Involvement	0.074	0.009	11.13**
Monitoring	0.103	0.018	21.53***
Control	0.070	0.004	4.54*
Familism	0.054		
Total variance in student grades explained by the independent variables is 3.1%.			
Third Generation Students[d]			
Involvement	0.179	0.063	66.47***
Monitoring	0.134	0.024	26.73***
Control	0.010		
Familism	−0.017		
Total variance in student grades explained by the independent variables is 8.7%.			

[a]$N = 3,571$. [b]$N = 1,352$. [c]$N = 1,180$. [d]$N = 994$.
*$p < .05$. **$p < .001$. ***$p < .0001$.

higher grades. Family involvement and family monitoring explained 4.5% of the total variance in the grades for all students. Family control and familism were not significant predictors of grades for the entire sample of students.

First generation model. Of the five variables entered, two emerged as significant predictors of grades for first generation students. Family involvement, $F(1, 1352) = 49.49$, $p < .0001$, and family monitoring, $F(2, 1351) = 29.19$, $p < .0001$) were positive predictors of grades for first generation students. Higher levels of family involvement and monitoring predicted higher grades for first generation students. Together they explained 4.1% of the total variance in *the grades of* first generation students. Family control and familism were not significant predictors of grades for first generation students.

Second generation model. The stepwise regression procedure for second generation students revealed three significant predictors of grades. Family involvement, $F(2, 1179) = 11.13$, $p < .001$, family monitoring $F(1, 1180) = 21.53$, $p < .0001$, and family control, $F(1, 1178) = 4.54$, $p < .05$, were positive predictors of grades for second generation students. Higher levels of family involvement, monitoring, and control predicted higher grades among second generation students. Together these variables explained 3.1% of the total variance in the grades of second generation students. Familism was not significant predictor of grades for second generation students.

Third generation model. For third generation students, stepwise regression analysis showed family involvement, $F(1, 994) = 66.47$, $p < .0001$, and family monitoring, $F(2, 993) = 26.73$, $p < .0001$, were significant predictors of grades. Higher levels of family involvement and family monitoring predicted higher grades for second generation students. These two variables explained 8.7% of the total variance in the grades of third generation students. Family control and familism were not significant predictors of grades for third generation students.

Discussion

There are several important findings in this study. First, there are significant generational differences in grades and perceptions of the family environment among Mexican American high school students. Also, for Mexican American high school students, family involvement and family monitoring are related to achievement as measured by grades. In the following paragraphs each of these findings will be discussed in greater detail. Finally, these findings will be discussed

in terms of their relevance to future research and public policy concerning the role of families in the education of Mexican American adolescents.

Generational Differences in Family Environment and Achievement

The finding that third generation students reported higher levels of family involvement than first or second generation students is interesting. Before attempting to explain this finding, it might be useful to reiterate the conceptual definition of family involvement in this study. Family involvement was defined as the extent to that parents and other family members attend or participate in school functions such as parent–teacher conferences and athletic events. In essence this variable is similar to popular notions of parent involvement, but extended to the entire family.

Given this definition, one explanation of this finding is that the parents of third generation students may be more familiar with the school system in the United States and are more prepared to participate in the educational process than the parents of first or second generation students. By definition, parents of first and second generation students are likely to be immigrants. It is important to point out that the reported levels of educational attainment for the parents of first and second generation students (8.6 and 9.1 years respectively) is considerably lower than for parents of third generation students (11.8 years). The difference in parents' educational attainment and the likelihood of their immigrant status may translate into less familiarity with the educational system and lower levels of involvement.

There is a second plausible explanation of this finding. It is also possible that greater levels of family involvement are due to acculturation. For the purpose of this article, the definition of acculturation is the acquisition of Euroamerican cultural values and practices. Immigrant parents of first and second generation students are less likely to have acculturated than the non-immigrant parents of third generation students. This explanation is consisted with previous research which has shown family functioning within Mexican American families is related to acculturation (Flores, 1982; Gonzalez, 1988; Rueschenberg and Buriel, 1989) In addition, the immigrant parents of first and second generation students may be less willing to participate in the educational process in order to be consistent with their cultural perspective of the role and status of teachers in the educational process (Valdes, 1996).

In turn, it is quite interesting, that third generation students reported lower grades than first or second generation students. Whereas third generation students reported more family involvement, first and second generation students reported higher student grades. This pattern of academic achievement is consistent with Suarez-Orozco and Suarez-Orozco (1995) who found that Mexican immigrant adolescents reported higher levels of academic achievement. Again, acculturation may play a significant role in this finding. The findings of Suarez-Orozco and Suarez-Orozco are consistent with other studies that also found first and second generation individuals are less acculturated or bicultural and have maintained traditional Mexican cultural values and practices (Buriel & Cardoza, 1988; Gandara, 1995).

Finally, first and second generation students reported higher levels of family monitoring than third generation students. This finding can also be attributed to the immigrant status and acculturation levels of students' parents and families. It is possible that other factors such as family monitoring, provide critical support for school achievement among first and second generation Mexican American adolescents.

In sum, although parents of first and second generation students are reportedly less involved in school, the students themselves reported higher grades than their third generation counterparts. It is possible that the immigrant status of parents and students and their level of acculturation explain generation differences in perceptions of family environment and achievement among Mexican American adolescents. It is also important to consider other family factors such as family monitoring which may help to explain the achievement of Mexican American adolescents.

The Relationship Between Family Environment and Achievement

Family involvement in education was a significant predictor of grades across all three generations of Mexican American high school students. Family monitoring was also a significant predictor of grades across all three generations of students. Finally, family control was a significant predictor of grades for second generation students.

The finding that family involvement and family monitoring was a significant predictor of grades consistently across all three generations is interesting given the previously discussed generational differences in levels of family involvement, monitoring, and grades reported by students. This finding is consistent with previous studies, which have found family support is linked to academic resilience and achievement (Alva, 1991; Gandara, 1995; Hernandez, 1993). There is clear and increasing support of the relationship between family support and achievement among Mexican Americans.

An examination of the findings of this study reveals that even though first and second generation students reported lower levels of family involvement, family involvement predicted grades for all three generations of students. Conversely, while first and second generation students reported significantly higher levels of family

monitoring, family monitoring predicted grades for all three generations of students

To fully understand the complexities of these findings, it would be helpful to more closely examine the impact of acculturation on students and their families. For example, first or second generation students who have not assimilated and maintained traditional cultural values may have coping mechanisms that allow them to navigate the schooling process. These coping mechanisms might be especially effective when students are confronted with difficult situations (such as being exposed to discrimination) or deficits in the educational system (such as being in a school with an inexperienced and underprepared group of teachers).

Also, lower levels of or the absence of family monitoring for students may lead to lower achievement. Although this study found that first generation students reported the highest levels of family monitoring and grades, it is unknown what might happen in families where monitoring exists at significantly lower levels. For later generation students who may have acculturated and acquired mainstream cultural values, factors such as family monitoring become more important and complement family involvement. In other words, as later generation students acculturate other forms of family support become increasingly important.

Implications for Policy, Research, and Practice

The findings of this study have implications for policymakers, researchers, and educators. First, policymakers, researchers, and educators must recognize that although family involvement is important to the achievement of Mexican American adolescents, differences in levels of involvement are not necessarily due to devaluation of education among Mexican American families. Rather, as has been previously discussed in this article, a number of cultural, acculturative, and experiential factors may impact the level of family involvement and academic achievement among Mexican Americans. Furthermore, the development and implementation of educational policies and programs that target Mexican American families should not be done uniformly across immigrant and later generations. The findings of this study reveal generational heterogeneity within the Mexican American community in regards to family involvement and achievement. Policymakers, researchers, and practitioners should work toward a greater understanding of this heterogeneity to increase the effectiveness of future efforts to increase family involvement and achievement among Mexican Americans.

Second, given the previous point, policymakers, researchers, and educators should ask themselves whether current models of parent involvement are appropriate and, in turn, effective for Mexican American families. The finding of this article suggests that different models of parent involvement might be necessary for different generations of Mexican American parents and adolescents. Also, as the heterogeneity within the group is better understood, parent involvement programs should be sensitive to the specific characteristics of the group. Furthermore, programs should incorporate mechanisms which utilize the group's strengths and which effectively meet the group's needs.

Finally, as part of the effort to understand the heterogeneity within the Mexican American community, alternative factors within the family should be considered for their impact on adolescents' development and educational success. Efforts to uncover and understand these family factors must be sensitive to the cultural parameters, which help shape the Mexican American family. Parent involvement in education among Mexican American families should be promoted while leaving the structure, values, and cultural practices of immigrant families intact. Immigrant families may, in part, provide cultural buffers and coping mechanisms, which promote the healthy adaptation and academic success of immigrant children and adolescents.

References

Alva, S. A. (1991). Academic invulnerability among Mexican–American students: The importance of protective resources and appraisals. *Hispanic Journal of Behavioral Sciences, 13*, 18–34.

Buriel, R., & Cardoza, D. (1988). Sociocultural correlates of achievement among three generations of Mexican American high school seniors. *American Educational Research Journal, 25*, 177–192.

Buriel, R., & De Ment, T. (1997). Immigration and sociocultural change in Mexican, Chinese, and Vietnamese American families. In A. Booth, A. C. Crouter, & N. Landale (Eds.). *Immigration and the family: Research and policy on U.S. immigrants.* (pp. 165–200). Mahwah, NJ: Lawrence Erlbaum Associates, Inc.

Delgado-Gaitan, C. (1991). Involving parents in the schools: A process of empowerment. *American Journal of Education, 100*, 20–46.

Delgado-Gaitan, C. (1994). Socializing young children in Mexican–American families: An intergenerational perspective. In P. M. Greenfield & R. R. Cocking (Eds.). *Cross-cultural roots of minority child development.* (pp. 55–86). Hillsdale, NJ: Lawrence Erlbaum Associates, Inc.

Dornbusch, S. M., Ritter, P. L., Leiderman, P. H., Roberts, D., & Fraleigh, M. (1987). The relation of parenting style to adolescent school performance. *Child Development, 58*, 1244–1257.

Dornbusch, S. M., Ritter, P. L., Mont-Reynaud, R., & Chen, Z. Y. (1990). Family decision making and academic performance in a diverse high school population. *Journal of Adolescent Research, 5*, 143–160.

Eccles, J. S., & Harold, R. D. (1996). Family involvement in children's and adolescents' schooling. In A. Booth & J. F. Dunn (Eds.). *Family-school links: How do they affect educational outcomes.* (pp. 3–34). Mahwah, NJ: Lawrence Erlbaum Associates, Inc.

Epstein, J. L. (1996). Perspective and previews on research and policy for school, family, and community partnerships. In A. Booth & J. F. Dunn (Eds.), *Family-school links: How do they affect educational outcomes.* (pp. 209–246). Mahwah, NJ: Lawrence Erlbaum Associates, Inc.

Flores, Y. G. (1982). *The impact of acculturation on the Chicano family: An analysis of selected variables.* Unpublished doctoral dissertation, University of California, Berkeley.

Gandara, P. (1995). *Over the ivy walls: The educational mobility of low-income Chicanos.* Albany, NY: SUNY Press.

García Coll, C., & Magnuson, K. (1997). The psychological experience of immigration: A developmental perspective. In A. Booth, A. C. Crouter, & N. Landale (Eds.). *Immigration and the family: Research and policy on U.S. immigrants.* (pp. 91–132). Mahwah, NJ: Lawrence Erlbaum Associates, Inc.

Gonzalez, R. R. (1988). *The impact of family support systems and strength of religious affiliation on levels of alienation and acculturation among Mexican American adolescents. Unpublished doctoral dissertation.* California School of Professional Psychology, Los Angeles.

Hernandez, L. P. (1993). *The role of protective factors in the school resilience of Mexican-American high school students.* Unpublished doctoral dissertation, Stanford University, CITY.

Rueschenberg, E., & Buriel, R. (1989). Mexican American family functioning and acculturation: A family systems perspective. *Hispanic Journal of Behavioral Sciences, 11*, 232–244.

Shavelson, R. J. (1996). *Statistical reasoning for the behavioral sciences* (3rd Edition). Boston, MA: Allyn & Bacon.

Suarez-Orozco, C., & Suarez-Orozco, M. (1995). *Transformations: Migrations, family life, and achievement motivation among Latino adolescents.* Stanford, CA: Stanford University Press.

Valdes, G. (1996). *Con respeto: Bridging the distances between culturally diverse families and schools.* New York: Teachers College Press.

Received November 23, 1999
Final revision received November 21, 2000
Accepted December 19, 2000

Applied Developmental Science
2002, Vol. 6, No. 2, 95–108

Integrating Normative Identity Processes and Academic Support Requirements for Special Needs Adolescents: The Application of an Identity-focused Cultural Ecological (ICE) Perspective

Joseph Youngblood II and Margaret Beale Spencer
University of Pennsylvania

The adolescent period continues to be a challenging phase of the life course. Irrespective of available economic resources, race, ethnicity and environmental supports, it is usually viewed as a burdensome period. The stage has special preparatory and historical relevance as youths move into young adulthood and the world of work. For particular periods of the life course, such as adolescence, developmental phases and transitions are unusually vulnerable, which makes prevention efforts more arduous although essential. Context quality and the importance of stable structural supports remain priority consideration, irrespective of the available economic resources. These themes are particularly relevant for youngsters deemed educationally or emotionally disabled. The responsibilities for maximizing youths academic performance, smoothing their transition from the early teen years, throughout middle and secondary schooling and into post-secondary training, and introducing them to the world of work are daunting developmental tasks. Accordingly, this article asserts the design and implementation of a contextually unique, culturally sensitive and educationally enhanced program and the application of an Identity-focused Cultural Ecological (ICE) intervention model designed to maximize the work skills, training, and educational outcomes of disabled adolescents and young adults.

Most basic human development and educational psychology textbooks agree that an individual begins developing a sense of self in infancy. However, the need for an achieved identity becomes the major developmental task at adolescence (e.g., Steinberg, 1999; Woolfolk, 1998). Identity formation processes during adolescence provide the anchor for adulthood and subsequent developmental tasks. Adolescence provides the first opportunity for individuals to wrestle with the anxiety-generating "Who am I?" question. Independent of gender, socioeconomic status, race and ethnicity, immigration status, and level of cognitive functioning, adolescents have the requisite, undergirding cognitive structures for an affective-based and differentiated response to one's evolving conceptualization of self. This dynamic self-assessing appraisal process is unavoidably influenced by the views of multiple others.

Identity formation includes the organization of abilities, beliefs, drives, and history into a consistent image of self. For some youth, in addition to the cognitive and physiologic associated influences, being burdened with the societal stereotyping accompanying an "at-risk" label often enhances the inherent challenges of the period. That is, struggling with a "difference as deficit" designation makes the task of arriving at a coherent sense of self and an achieved identity more complex and difficult, at best. As a worst case, however, for youth requiring *special supports*, the character of the "evolving sense of self" process is perilous and requires careful consideration in the planning of programs and the structuring of supports. The task requires broadened conceptualizations of identity processes which explicitly address sociocultural themes and ecological character. An identity-focused cultural-ecological (ICE) perspective provides a comprehensive way of thinking about and implementing best practices for obtaining commonly valued outcomes. For youth, generally agreed upon life course relevant outcomes include academic achievement, preparation for post-secondary training and schooling, exposure to and preparation for productive career options and opportunities for apprenticeship experiences, which lead to the acquisition of stable work.

Support for the research reported in this article was provided by the Casey and Ford Foundations and the Office of Educational Research Improvement (OERI) awarded to Margaret Beale Spencer, along with resources made available by the Center for Community Partnerships (University of Pennsylvania), Philadelphia Public School System, and the National Organization on Disability.

Requests for reprints should be sent to Joseph Youngblood II, University of Pennsylvania, 3440 Market Street, Suite 500, Philadelphia, PA 19104–3325. E-mail: youngbli@dolphin.upenn.edu

The Phenomenological Variant of Ecological Systems Theory (PVEST) (Spencer, 1995, 1999; Swanson, Spencer & Petersen, 1998), the undergirding framework for an identity-focused cultural ecological (ICE) perspective, reinforces the importance of simultaneously considering:

1. The special *risk factors*,
2. *The net effects of supports versus experienced stressors*,
3. The *reactive coping strategies* employed, and
4. The *emergent identities manifested*.

In this framework, all are critical components and mediators for obtaining the commonly valued life course outcomes noted above (refer to Figure 1).

As noted in the model described in Figure 1, the specific developmental outcomes frequently observed at adolescence only provide and exacerbate subsequent risk as one transitions out of adolescence and into adulthood. More specific, youths' failure to leave the adolescent period with a positive achieved identity serves to exacerbate the level of risk as they transition into adulthood, where they must find productive solutions to normative adulthood developmental tasks (e.g., see Swanson et al., 1998). Given these circumstances more appropriate structuring and conceptualizing of schooling experiences for special needs youth should result in better outcomes such as school completion and adequate preparation for adulthood tasks (Spencer, 1999; Swanson, Spencer et al., 1998).

Environmental Risks, Supports and Normative Adolescent Development Themes Considered From a Phenomenological Variant of Ecological Systems Theory (PVEST) Perspective

Adolescence is a potentially difficult period for most youth. Erikson (1968) describes the period's normative identity crisis as one involving the exploration of many new roles in preparation for adulthood. The difficulties of this developmental task are heightened for poor inner-city minority youth who, while dealing with normative maturational issues, must confront issues such as discrimination, school failure and violence. This is even more challenging for inner-city youth classified as educationally or emotionally disabled.

Spencer, Dupree, and Hartmann (1997) suggest that youths' experiences in different cultural contexts (e.g., home, school, peer group, community) influence their perception of self. This statement could be construed solely to mean that there is a strong relationship between the experiences of youth and their self-esteem. Spencer (1999) expands this assertion by indicating

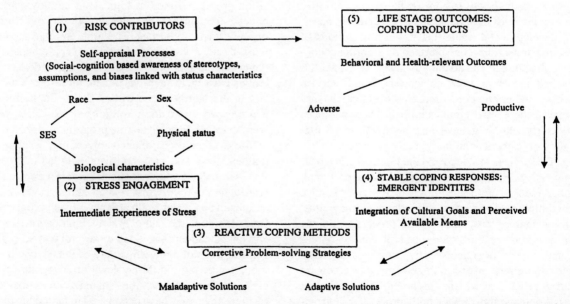

Figure 1. Spencer's Phenomenological Variant of Ecological Systems Theory (PVRST) (See Spencer, 1997, 1999). From the perspective of this framework, the educational context for youth who are minority group members or special needs youths fails its charges in almost all of these areas. As described elsewhere (see Spencer, 1999), too frequently educational settings themselves provide significant sources of risk; that is, they do not represent trustworthy places and "safe havens" for learning which requires engaging in intellectual risk taking. In and of themselves, they do not provide support adequate to offset the inherent stress level. In addition, traditional schooling experiences do not provide models of adaptive coping strategies, thus, maladaptive coping methods are honed with dire consequences. Subsequently and consistent with Erikson's (1968) views concerning the role of negative identities for more general ego functioning, emergent identities become ingrained, and are manifest across settings and opportunities.

that the processing of phenomena and experiences not only determines how much one feels valued or valuable (e.g., self-esteem), but it also affects the meaning assigned to different aspects of "self" (e.g., abilities, physical attributes, behaviors, activities). More specifically, Spencer et al. (1997) suggested that it is not merely the experience but its *perception* in different cultural contexts, which influences how one perceives and experiences the self. Their analyses suggest that educators must aid these students toward alternative perceptual and adaptive coping processes, and the development of new identities to reverse the education and life outcome trends currently experienced by this population. The transformative supports needed from educators and associated responsive changes required from students should afford positive options for students' with ascribed "at risk" status to successfully transition through myriad environmental stresses.

Few efforts examine the range of achievement levels within low-socioeconomic and minority status groups which, if considered, would aid our knowledge concerning resiliency and its prediction among low resource groups (e.g., Connell, Spencer & Aber (1994), Nettles, 1991; Spencer, Cole, Dupree, Glymph & Pierre, 1993). As expected, the situation is more dire for those deemed educationally and/or emotionally disabled. Research on poor and minority youth, especially those considered educationally or emotionally disabled, have infrequently considered the contexts and explored the complexity of urban settings. Scholarly inquiries generally fail to address the structural influences on the lives of adolescents at particularly unsettling developmental points that is, during periods of normative transitions characterized by significant cognitive, physiologic and social upheaval. Relevant contexts and resources such as schools, social service agencies, and public policy initiatives (potential "supportive partners") are left unexamined. These contexts, particularly schooling, have the potential for maximizing the "fit" between the individual student characteristics, the services provided and the jointly desired academic and social outcomes. An important aspect of an identity-focused cultural ecological (ICE) perspective is the critical role of context for understanding youths' meaning making processes. These processes include how they perceive and experience risk, assess sources of support, and organize reactive coping responses. Their coping responses are linked to stable emergent identity processes which, as noted, are persistent across contexts and predict both productive and adverse outcomes. Therefore, improving the educational experiences for special needs and at-risk students enhances the quality of education for all students. Altering intrusive and unsupportive school effects can have important implications for the responsive coping behaviors of students, mediating identity processes, and the consequent outcomes of; academic achievement, school completion, and productive post-secondary options, so important for adolescence to young adulthood transitions.

SOS Program Overview—A PVEST Driven Model

The Start-on-Success Scholars (SOS) internship project is an exploration, demonstration, and evaluation of diverse expressions of resiliency and vulnerability among disabled, urban adolescents. The internship project's aim is to implement and evaluate the effectiveness of an intervention strategy designed for this population group. Specifically, the program is designed to enhance the expression of resiliency (generally defined as manifested health and mastery demonstrated under conditions of chronic risk) in disabled youth transitioning from school to the world of work and independent living (Spencer, 1999).The SOS program services special education students between 9th and 12th grade who attend one of two feeder West Philadelphia high schools. All of the students identified themselves as African American or Hispanic of African descent and all of the students were classified as being in need of special education for academic–learning or emotional disabilities. Classifications include Serious Emotional Disturbance (SED), Learning Disabled (LD), Educable Mentally Retarded (EMR) and Trainable Mentally Retarded (TMR). Students in the SOS program were involved in a school-to-work transition program aimed at improving employment and education outcomes for inner-city youth with learning or emotional disabilities. The program consisted of a work-based training experience that supplemented students' regular school program. Students worked and attended class on the campus of a major research university in the Northeastern United States. In addition to learning work transition and job related skills, youth were involved in an academic program designed to increase academic proficiency in reading, writing and mathematics. The program also included courses in Professional Development and Service Learning designed to improve work related skills, interpersonal competencies, and self-efficacy. The program is funded through the school system, Foundation support, and job placements provided by several partner organizations, including the University of Pennsylvania. Although showing a different level of academic "prowess" and persistence, the students are considered resilient since they have persevered in their educational activities, despite being enrolled in special educational or socioemotional focused special needs classrooms. In addition, more often than not, these students reside in economically stressed families.

Ordinarily, such youngsters dropout of or fail to complete secondary school, whereas the special education classification label and placement too often further exacerbate the degree of risk and vulnerability. The general expectation is that such youngsters will become "dependent adults" since the majority will be unable to take on adult work-world related roles and responsibilities.

One goal of the SOS program demonstration is to afford paid apprenticeship opportunities and off-(school) campus classes with uniquely committed teachers and sensitive supports. As previously noted, the goal is to use specific service delivery strategies and supports to foster a powerful programming model and then evaluate its effectiveness for potential replication in other parts of the nation.

Young people with limited financial commitments and familial obligations (although this changes as young people take on adulthood roles like parenting) who have poor engagement experiences with the labor market are the most at-risk of developing what Rodriguez (1997) describes as learned universal helplessness. This learned helplessness attributes external cause as the reason young people are not having better success finding consistent employment. Consequently, aggressive attitudes or behaviors toward society are produced. These attitudes influence how students view the larger labor market, thus further alienating them from mainstream society. In addition, such attitudes potentially put young people in direct confrontation with the justice system, which could further limit or inhibit opportunities to secure stable employment.

Given what we know about the maladaptive effects of this experience on young people transitioning into adulthood roles concerning their physiological, psychological, and emotional well being it is clear that more needs to be done to assist students with special needs to better effectively negotiate, acquire, and maintain stable and viable employment opportunities.

In response to many of these concerns, the SOS project was created by the Philadelphia Public School System and assisted by Foundation support to aid special needs youths, particularly those residing in the West Philadelphia community in their efforts to move from school to viable employment options. The School District of Philadelphia, the National Organization on Disability (NOD) and their partners (e.g., University of Pennsylvania faculty members and staff) collectively designed the project to afford specific opportunities for adolescents and young adults. Students with disabilities at a local high school are provided with sets of coordinated activities, such as service learning, a professional development seminar, and peer mediation, along with supported academic instruction and varied work experience. The programming and apprenticeship increases youths' options for employment and post secondary training. Thus, the SOS program strives "to beat the odds" of unemployment and under-employment associated with minority status and disability for West Philadelphia's disabled citizens by specialized supportive programming for adolescent high school students.

The SOS program attempts to help disenfranchised youth with disabilities respond to the many challenges of inner-city life through the development of healthy daily and long term coping skills. An important SOS element is the promotion of student achievement through expectation-setting and success-recognition. Clearly stated expectations and standards are defined with the assistance of the principal, teachers, parents, researchers, business–industry representatives, and post-secondary educators. Consequently, students develop appropriate competencies, skills and attitudes, which then assist them in making smooth transitions into adult roles, such as the family, community, workplace, or future educational endeavors.

SOS academic goals and objectives for student learning include the following characteristics:

- Meeting graduation requirements towards a high school diploma—Pennsylvania requires special needs students to graduate based on specifications stated in their Individual Education Plans (IEP);
- Incorporating high expectations for attendance, academic performance, behavioral standards, service learning and career development;
- Providing two year school-to-work apprenticeships for 100% of its students; and
- Parental involvement through initial group meetings and individualized meetings throughout students' program participation.

The instructional program and curriculum framework design model state and national standards, along with core competencies of successful school-to-work programs; examples include guidelines from the National School-To-Career Center; and national, local, and regional drop out recovery models. Furthermore, SOS is grounded in a well documented theoretical framework, namely Spencer's (1995, 1999) PVEST, which explains human motivation and behavior in relation to multiple contexts, including both classroom achievement and career development settings (see Figure 1). Most important, the theory represents an ICE perspective.

In response to the need for innovative and sensitive teaching methods and service delivery for this population of students, additional components were added to the SOS curriculum that specifically addressed classroom performance, dropping out, feelings of helplessness, preparation for the world of work, and the need for effective transitioning. All are common themes for low-income students with disabilities.

The SOS curriculum centers on core subjects: Vocational English, Business–Consumer Mathematics, Service Learning, Professional Development, and Work

Transition. Each academic subject encompasses the following objectives:

- Curriculum Integration—learning in the context of career majors or special interests, curriculum integration within and across disciplines, project–work-based and thematic learning, career clusters, school-based learning and connecting activities;
- High Academic Standards—raising student achievement, academic standards and skill standards, effective assessment methods and instruments;
- Instructional Technology—using technology and multi-media to enhance learning, distance learning, Internet access and usage, electronic communication and portfolios;
- Multiple Partnerships—fostering school, community and business partnerships, secondary and post-secondary linkages, work-based learning, adult mentors, career guidance, student internships, and constant parent and community involvement (performance feedback toward continuous improvement with all of the partners noted is an integral part of the process of the design and implementation of the project);
- Supportive Learning Environments—teaching career skills in a real life context, career awareness, exploration and preparation, alternative scheduling, and classroom size.

As a theory-driven instructional framework, the program design enables students to develop skills that are essential for deciding on a career, obtaining a job, and being prepared for professional and occupational advancement.

Through its use of a developmentally appropriate, culturally competent, and contextually relevant perspective, SOS is able to provide an effective and unique academic–work-based learning experience for young people with special needs who are expected to transition into adulthood roles. Traditionally such groups are undeserved by conventional school-to-work initiatives. SOS effectively demonstrates how students with special needs respond to enhanced supports designed specifically to assist in the transition from school to the world of work. It also provides a significant challenge to traditional assumptions regarding the career development behavior of at-risk, special needs minority youth populations.

This program initiative sees the individual developing transferable skills that will allow one to function highly in an independent environment. One of the main purposes of the curriculum is to assist the student in recognizing and overcoming social and physical areas of underdevelopment. From this perspective, the curriculum addresses environmental barriers to career development and encourages individuals to explore beliefs not only about themselves, but also about their environment. Examination of interests, performance, and expectations are initial starting point, while improving abstract reasoning, social perspectives, and interpersonal problem solving represent ongoing themes.

SOS Developmental Framework

Consistent with an ICE perspective, students are asked to describe and build upon their own identity. Students are encouraged to think in terms of their multiple self-referents (e.g., African–American and male or African–American and female). The meaning of these roles are discussed at length. Background factors are discussed (e.g., urban vs. rural, wealthy vs. working class) and related to the type of learning opportunities students experience. The importance of seeking out new environments for new learning is also emphasized.

1. Life Events

Both personal and social life events are examined to illustrate their continual impact on career development and opportunity. This is an effort to emphasize the interplay between a person's environment and behavior. The goal is to help students develop a balanced view of themselves, their responsibilities, and the events that have shaped their lives.

2. Lessons: "Things learned"

This component emphasizes the connection between learning and behavior, both adaptive and maladaptive, and their relationship to personal expectations and outcomes.

3. Identity Question: "What am I?"

This component examines self-efficacy, outcome expectations, interests, values and skills. The goal is to develop cognitive structure for understanding the self in relation to the world of work.

4. Expectations and Aspirations: "What I'd like to do?"

Having a disability does not erase goals and personal aspirations. This component focuses on choice of short and long term goals and actions. Students develop resumes, cover letters, and develop career plans and strategies.

SOS Service Learning

The term "service learning" describes the process by which SOS students learn and develop through active participation in organized service experiences that meet actual community needs. Researchers, such as Duckenfield and Swanson (1992), found a significant link between service learning, resilience, and drop-out prevention among "at-risk" youth. These activities provide students with opportunities to use newly acquired skills and knowledge in real-life situations with-in their communities. Service learning is integrated into students' academic curriculum as structured time for students to think, talk, and write about what they did and experienced during the service activity. Therefore, service learning enhances student classroom learning by providing a context for immediate appreciation of student knowledge beyond the classroom and into the community. Finally, service learning helps foster the development of a sense of community and connectedness.

SOS participants' "normative" self-concepts and values are used to enhance their involvement in service learning by framing it as a personal challenge or showing the students how they are needed by others. Service learning enables students to experience developmentally appropriate adaptive outcomes, such as personal growth, social growth, intellectual growth, citizenship, and preparation for the world of work.

The Service Learning Component also provides opportunities for participants to work with peer mentors, community advocates, and former SOS graduate mentors. These experiences enhance the possibility of SOS participants to develop adaptive coping strategies by providing successful models of behaviors that can be applied as work identities become more salient. Consistent with a PVEST framework, the service-learning component of the SOS programs provides students with an opportunity to become resource providers–givers as opposed to being only resource takers. In that context, service learning also increases the likelihood that students will engage in help-seeking behavior.

SOS mentoring component. Teachers and SOS staff, in conjunction with work site mentors, develop a system in which second year participants mentor first year participants. Second year participants are given minor supervisory tasks including reporting of hr and absences. In addition, second year participants assist in training first year participants assigned where the second year participants are currently working or have worked the previous year. Second year participants are also responsible for weekly meetings with their first year mentees. Mentors and mentees are also expected to engage in peer learning and tutoring and are assigned group projects that require on-going collaboration.

SOS community service component. Students, parents, teachers, SOS staff, and mentors develop Individualized Community Service Programs (ICSP) for all first year participants. SOS participants select a community service activity site-based on individual needs, talents, and interests and are expected to engage in the community service activities for the duration of their apprenticeship. A Community Service Board (CSB), which is student run and operated, is created to monitor mandatory student service hours (e.g., 4 hr per month), and assist teachers in collecting data for student evaluation in areas of community service. Students are responsible for keeping community service journals. The CSB meets on a monthly basis and reflects on members' experiences and their impact on the community. The community service component, much like the service learning component, helps SOS scholars to develop an identity that is linked to their role of being a community resource provider or "helper." In addition, SOS students have an opportunity to interact with and become a part of the community as a whole, thus potentially reducing many of the intermediate experiences of stress created by neighborhood risk contributors.

SOS post-graduate visiting lecture series (PVLS). This lecture series was introduced in the second year of the program. Initial implementation utilized former SOS participants speaking to groups of current participants about a multiplicity of issues and topics, including the SOS experience, job hunting, "real" job experiences, marketability, upward mobility, and job retention. PVLS contributes to SOS by providing current participants with a realistic understanding of the world of work from their peers' point of view. PVLS also allows the SOS staff to review the program and make changes based on the successes and impediments experienced by past participants, and it provides the evaluation team with critical follow-up data. PVLS enables SOS scholars to have meaningful dialogue with peers and creates an additional layer of support for both groups of SOS scholars.

SOS Professional Development Seminar (PDS)

The Professional Development Seminar (PDS) concentrates on preparing students for life after high school. Using PVEST as a framework, SOS students are exposed to the challenges and expectations that will confront them in their families, communities and larger society. Through a variety of activities students complete the following:

- All certification process requirements for program and post secondary employment.

Such requirements include, but are not limited to, developing an up-to-date resume, acquiring three letters of recommendation for potential employment or advanced training or both and completing three off-site job interviews with perspective employers.

- All paperwork for student portfolios.

This includes a Career Decision Making inventory (CDM), Future Planning Inventory, student interview survey, vocational assessment, parent interview survey, former teacher interview survey, and release information forms.

- All paperwork and applications for local and state funded resources and potential employment agencies.

Students and their parent(s) or guardian(s) are required to complete the following: applications materials for the Office of Vocational Rehabilitation (OVR), the Office of Mental Health or Mental Retardation (OMH or MR), and an application and test for admissions to the Community College of Philadelphia (CCP).

- Develop a Post Secondary Action Plan (PSAP).

A PSAP consists of a portfolio of students' accomplishments, certifications, awards, up-to-date resumes, and individualized 5-year plans to be used as interview aids for students looking for post-secondary training and employment.

- All testing associated with program evaluation and development.

PDS is closely tied to the Service Learning component of the SOS program. A portion of the program activities include public speaking opportunities designed to develop and hone communication and interviewing skills along with a deeper understanding of appropriate professional and informal behavior. In addition, students participate in activities that examine workforce realities such as limited job opportunities for low resource areas; perceptions of opportunity structure after high school; the importance of developing and recognizing transferable skills for future job acquisition; occupational stereotypes, realistic occupational goals; personal deficits; the impact of behavior on future expectations; expectations from family and community and other barriers to employment.

Research Questions and Theoretical Linkages

The work described here represents an identity-focused cultural ecological (ICE) perspective, which is heavily dependent upon social-cognitive perceptual processes. Its foundation is phenomenological, which suggests that it is impossible to understand behavior except as experienced by the individual. The approach taken is driven by the PVEST, illustrated in

Figure 1. This model represents a sequential process across the life course, in which life stage specific risks are linked to the net effect of supports versus stress. The net level of stress experienced is conceptualized as associated with the person's reactive coping strategy employed which can be either adaptive (e.g., school engagement) or maladaptive (e.g., truancy). As a function of redundant deployment, the particular reactive strategy becomes stabilized across contexts and internalized as an identity. The identity becomes associated with particularly patterned outcomes. For any developmental stage, the outcomes further exacerbate the subsequent stage's level of risk. Thus, the model demonstrates a particular life-course temporality in sequenced deployment across the life course. This sequence is deployed in developmentally consistent ways literally "from the cradle to the coffin" (see Dupree, Spencer, & Bell, 1997; Spencer, 1995, 1999; Spencer et al., 1997; Swanson, Spencer, & Petersen, 1998). Qualitative data from the SOS program evaluation are used here to demonstrate the model's efficacy for directing intervention efforts. Ethnographic findings collected from the SOS program evaluation are presented for two purposes. First, data are utilized for demonstrating the program's ability to *decrease* the deployment of maladaptive reactive coping methods (e.g., lack of an on-task academic orientation) as a consequence of the net impact of perceived support versus stress for a group of high risk urban students. Second, ethnographic data demonstrate the acquisition of new identities from an intervention designed to impact the linkage between the deployment of maladaptive coping strategy and new emergent identities (e.g., school valuing and sense of agency). Both linkages are connected to school performance outcomes.

The overall program evaluation included both quantitative and qualitative methods. To demonstrate the program's link to an ICE Perspective, the authors relied heavily on qualitative data obtained from ethnographic field notes, teacher and mentor interviews, parent and student focus group interviews, and student exit interviews.

The qualitative interview protocol, like the SOS program content, are guided by Spencer's (1995) PVEST model and seek to examine patterns of resiliency and identity development in the above referenced population. Ethnographic data reported represent exemplar findings from exit interviews with an interviewer and SOS scholars. Questions cover a variety of subjects including their perceptions of how the program has benefited them, noted sources of support both from job site staff members and teachers. Experiences of stress from home, school and job site, and their views of how and if the program has aided them as compared with prior non-program experiences are presented.

Interests in the Program: Self Cognitions of Risk and Net Level Support versus Stress

The interviewer begins the exit interview by asking about perceptions of risk and support versus stressors.

Interviewer: So why did you want to be in the program?

Katrina: They had a lot of choices and plus I didn't want ... I mean, school is really not for me and I just thought the best thing to do was to ... dropping out and not going to school. Well this program, it did, it saved me. That's why I wanted to be in this program and I have a lot of opportunities. It's a lot of opportunities in here. It's a change, it's different, it's not the same as in school, you know. The change is good, that's what I like.

Angel (Male): Well it seem like the program had good things that I could use in the future like get training, training I can't get over there at Piney Ridge [high school pseudonym] ... And I wanted to be with more professional people, you know, people who are serious about their work and teach me a couple of things.

Interviewer: ... And what have you actually learned?

Angel (Male): I learned a lot of things. Everything has improved. My mathematics has improved. My reading, because I was a little slow in reading also. I learned how to work with grown ups and, you know, basically just work with more computers, because when I was over at Piney Ridge [pseudonym], we worked in computers but not like for money and things like that, not for business, just music.

Consistent with a PVEST framework, perceptions of risk and stresses and supports are unavoidably associated with the character of the context: In this case, specifically, Piney Ridge High School students' discourse indicate no gender differences in acknowledging the links between recognized risks and perceptions of context-linked supports versus stressors.

Linkages Between Net Level Support Versus Stress and Reactive Coping Strategy

Interviewer: Would you say that you were performing well at Piney Ridge High School prior to entering the SOS Program?

Angel V. (Male): I can't say. Well, because, I got left down. I was being a rascal or, you know, cutting and doing what I wasn't suppose to be doing. (Interviewer probes) ... Yeah, you know the teachers just gave me work and explaining it and then I just did it and left the class or just didn't go to class period. That's why I said Mr. A (teacher) and Mr. Y (teacher) really helped me out a lot, because you know, Mr. A speak professionally all the time and Mr. Y professionally all the time. He always speaks clear and make sure that everybody understands what he means even though he says long words. He make sure everybody understands. And if you have a problem, then he'll tell you straight up. He's not going to be like, go to the principal or go ... He just tell you straight up, you know, either you fix it or we got to work something out.

Rashae (Male): (Shaking his head no. Explains) At Piney Ridge I was. I had friends over there and friends that didn't care and I didn't care. So I would just run in the halls and doing the things that I wanna do. But over here at SOS Program, people they care and I think it's no way that you can cut classes over here. You have to come to class.

Interviewer: What do you mean you can't cut class?

Rashae (Male): Well over here, I mean, you don't ... If you go to work, then you have to come to class, but if you don't go to work or you come to class, you have to call out and say you wasn't coming in or ... But at Piney, you can just leave out the classroom and just go.

Coping with the net level of stress not offset by a similar level of support is a normal human response. That is, to survive requires deploying reactive coping strategies, which may be either maladaptive in character or adaptive. The students' responses are revealing and illustrative demonstrations of reactive coping responses which are linked to context character.

Interviewer: What were the differences, if any, between attending class at Piney and participating in the SOS program?

Christopher: When you at Piney School, people make fun of you. But when you here, nobody won't say nothing cause you got other people in there that's in the same situation you in.

Angel V. (Male): At Piney Ridge it was a lot more ... whole lot of people and mostly everybody are clowns. Most of them are clowns. Over here, you know, everybody learn to grow up a little bit more than at Piney Ridge, I did what everybody else did which was a bad influence. Piney Ridge is a bad influence. It was a bad influence for me. So I just keep on doing it, you know. Here it's good influence and now I'm doing pretty good and if I go back to Piney Ridge, I'm going to keep the good influence.

Rashae (Male): Well, at Piney Ridge, in the class that you have, it's like 36 students, whatever, in the class at Piney Ridge. But in the program in the SOS Program...Interviewer: So what does that mean about 36 students?

Rashae (Male): Well it's only one teacher in there and in the SOS Program, it's only like 14 kids in class, whatever, and the teachers can go around to everyone and see where everyone need help on, or students help each other. But at Piney Ridge, everyone, they like selfish. They wouldn't help and things ... The SOS Program is better than Piney Ridge.

Interviewer: What makes you ... Why do you think there's a difference between the student helping each other in this program and not helping each other at Piney?

Rashae (Male): Because they're ... Well half of them over there criminal. They're like they just got out of jail or whatever. I mean, they just ... I think Piney Ridge like a school for bad kids.

Interviewer: So why do you think they're more likely to help you over here?

Rashae (Male): Because everybody over here nice. They don't think about just they self. Think about other people in the class and ... Well we help one another in the class work or out of class.

Evident here is that Rashae's "emergent identity" as a resource provider and support is evident. As the following discourse suggests, students know when they are not being taught and the fact is a source of significant stress.

Interviewer: What differences, if any, do you find between the level of instruction and interaction that you had with your teachers at Piney versus what you have with your teachers in the SOS Program? And you talked about it ... somewhat up here (referring to notes) ... when you said ... the 36 students ... but go in to a little more detail. What does that mean being in the class with one teacher and 36 students?

Rashae (Male): Well the teacher won't be able to get around to everyone. She has to stop in between. Before she gets to you, she has to stop, talk to that student and stop and talk to that one and by then, you be like, never mind. So you just get tired of the hollering out her name, whatever. Then she tell you be quiet or whatever. And you be quiet, you be sitting there and get the wrong answers. You be sitting there and won't know what to write down or put down, or the other, if you and Miss D (teacher), two other teachers, then this person go around and help you with that

person or whatever or if you need help, you call one of the other teachers over there.

Angel V. (Male): Well, teachers over here, they make sure that you understand everything. Over there, they gave it to you and you understand it. Well maybe you ask one question or two, but if you ask too many questions, then they'll get mad. Over here, you can ask as many questions as you feel as long as they know that you start understanding better and better every time they tell you. And they care more automatically. Over there, there's a whole lot of students, so they really don't care that (much) ... you know. They just give you the work and make sure, you know ... Give you the grade. Over here, they help you out.

Students appear to be quite clear concerning the linkages between the character of the context, the net level of stress versus support, and attendant reactive coping strategies deployed in response. This awareness applies both to the home and school contexts. The level and quality of stress experienced is also exacerbated by the fact that support (e.g., counseling) is often neither available nor considered a source of support. Students appear to understand the importance of having a "safe environment" for maximizing the use of learning opportunities.

Interviewer: What are the differences, if any, in the learning atmosphere at Piney Ridge versus the learning atmosphere at SOS? And by atmosphere, I mean like ... actually the physical presence in terms of being on "P" [a major northeastern university] campus versus being at the school. What it means, you know, not having to interact with ... for example, you talked about, you know, how bad the kids are over there. So what are some differences in terms of the atmosphere?

Katrina: At Piney you free. You free to do what you wanna do. It's your choice. You leave and it shouldn't be like that, because you leave, I mean, who cares? Half of the teachers don't even know your name over there. So it's just like you come, you leave, it's your decision. But over here, it's like people care about you. If you not here, they calling you, you know. They making you wanna come. They making you wanna get a education, not just saying, oh well, if she don't want it, then she won't have it. No, it's not like that in here. They gonna give it to you. If you don't want, they still gonna give it to you.

Katrina's response suggests significant "self valuing" by teachers and other SOS staff. As the interviewer's questions become more focused, it is easy to capture the specifics of the reactive coping strategies deployed with respect to perceiving stress versus support. There is consistent evidence of new emergent identities.

Adolescents must transition between contexts and find ways to integrate their various experiences within each context. As a context, the "traditional" school setting was a source of stress engagement for the SOS student participants. Students frequently cited the dissonance producing-experiences at Piney Ridge as being factors that limited their desire to engage in the learning process. When examined closely, students were able to identify several contextual stressors, including perceived peer unpopularity and perceived negative teacher perceptions. This analysis is critical to our understanding of the risks and stressors that contribute to the different coping methods deployed by students across contexts.

Interviewer: What changes, if any, have you noticed in your own behavior that you would attribute to leaving Piney Ridge High and coming in to the SOS Program? What changes have you seen in yourself?

Christopher: When I was at Piney … wasn't doing no work. If I was at Piney now, I probably be in the hall somewhere with somebody or running around. Probably being chased by the NTA's (Non-Teaching Assistants – School Security) … (In response to question … What changed that?) … Everybody's like, you know what I mean. You made a contract and then you got to go by it. If you don't do it … what they say, you going to go back to Piney and you don't wanna go over there, cause you ain't going to learn nothing. So we rather stay here and deal with the consequences.

Interviewer: What are some of the things or factors about the program (which) helped you change? Like what are some things about the program that you think helped you change?

Christopher: You be like, you in class with same people you see everyday, you understand. So you get used to seeing they faces and it don't really matter no more who you read in front of (… in response to the specific components of the program that helped) … Because you got … you know what I mean, you got choices, you know what I mean, if you want to succeed and make the money. You know what I'm saying? You going to do it anyway, but if you wanna be sit there and be broke, that's on you. You know what I mean? Just ain't going to have no money. Will be somebody always borrowing something from somebody or you going to be hustling.

Rashae (Male): Well things that I was. Responsibility at home and really class work for me to learn. Like your mind learn what the world is about. That you should think about what's gonna be in the future and not the past.

Interviewer: What would you say was the purpose of the professional development component of the program and how would that information benefit you? That's Mr. A's class.

Katrina: How did his class help me? His class has a lot of reading, a lot of writing, studying, going to the library back and forth. It just kept you on the go. If you didn't get nothing out of it, then that's you, but it just kept me on the run. Library and this and going to dif … It just kept me going to different places. Like I wanna be a nurse, you know, and I went to the nursing. I went down to the nursing place down Thompson. [Hall] I got my … So I talk to them a little bit about it. So they gave me some … I asked them some questions. They gave me some answers about it. So it helped me a whole lot.

Interviewer: Before getting into the program, what did you plan to do after graduation?

Angel (Male): Armed Forces … Maybe after I'm out the Forces, then I probably look for a good paying job or go to college. Because right now, you don't have to go to college first and then go to the navy. Right now, you go straight to the navy and they give you college courses there and when you're out, then you can go to another college if you want or a training school like DPT Business School or … Just keep on learning.

Katrina: Before getting into this program? You mean being back at school? I was not going to school, so I know that I wouldn't … Well you know what I thought I wasn't even gonna graduate this year or no year. I thought I wasn't even, you know… I wasn't even probably qualify to graduate, that's how I felt, you know. This program help me to feel good about myself and accept myself no matter, you know, how … What I can't do, cause I can always try, you know, just give my best. And if my best ain't good, then …

Not just experiences in school but other contexts such as home and family compromise productive coping responses and life stage specific outcomes. Significant "assaults" accompany urban life and take their "toll" on psychic energy available for academic achievement.

Interviewer: During the school year, describe any personal problems or conflicts that you had. And by this I mean, did you have any problems in your home or personal life? Did you have the death of a family member or friend? Did you become a parent or are you an expectant parent? Were you arrested or any of your family members? Have you had any altercations? Any of those things. Any problems?

Katrina: Well, yeah, my little niece had passed away. So, you know, that affected ... That affected me.

Interviewer: How old was she?

Katrina: She was 6 months.

Interviewer: Oh, no. That's right, I do remember when that happened. How did that affect you?

Katrina: Well it's like she was here one day and the next day, she was gone. So it shocked me in a way, cause you know, I went to school, came back home and somebody told me and my mom telling me that my little niece died. I'm like, what? So it was just shocking that's all.

Interviewer: (Katrina had previously discussed a difficult situation with her brother) What about like this situation with your brother? How did that ...

Katrina: Well that situation, I'm sill is angry, you know, cause he only 17 and I wouldn't think nothing like that would happen for him, you know, being 30 (inaudible). So I'm still angry about that, because of the fact that the guy is a grown man. So I'm still upset about that. I feel like doing something myself, but I don't wanna, you know. I don't wanna do that.

Interviewer: Did any of those personal problems interfere with your academics? In terms of coming to school, wanting to do the work.

Katrina: Well, coming to school, yeah. A little and coming to school, cause I stayed out, you know, a lot.

More important, not just academic relevant coping behaviors were reported as altered but also social behaviors. Relationships and social behaviors continue to be salient independent of task: Many skills and tasks are both social interaction and academic (skill) achievement relevant. Relatedly, the adolescents appear very aware of the critical role of language, its context linkages, and its ability to inhibit and support opportunities across settings.

Interviewer: Do you think your social skills changed from the beginning of the year until the end? For example, you know, in terms of being able to talk to people, interact with people. Do you think you've seen a change in yourself from the time class first started until now?

Rashae (Male): Yes.

Interviewer: How so?

Rashae: Because when I first started the class, I was talking like everybody else in the class.

Like everybody else talking street slang and different ways you know what I mean... and other things like that. And I just think ... Well I always wanted to talk straight but it's just that I was just hanging around the wrong group and they was teaching me how to talk different, street wise.

Interviewer: Now, the point is, I've heard you say on several occasions, you know ... (about the importance of) ... talking straight. What have you learned about ... Is that ... ever appropriate? Is it ever appropriate to use slang if you're in your neighborhood or if you're talking with your friends?

Rashae (Male): Not really.

Interviewer: You' don't think it's ever appropriate if that's how you interact with your buddies and everything? Do you think that's appropriate versus ... Or do you draw distinctions between talking one way on the job site and then maybe being able to talk another way when you interact with your friends? Explain ...

Rashae (Male): Well when you're talking with your friends, you can talk anyway you want cause that's not ... You not going to a job interview or you not talking to somebody that's like really important. I mean that you should be talking (inaudible ... about) your job, but after a while you should get on your mind that you going to a job interview tomorrow or whatever, so you should maybe like, sit in the room by yourself and talk (inaudible). I mean, like you in the job interview and show your eye contact or whatever. Get somebody that's in your family, whatever, like try to think about what you gonna tell them or whatever. The words you're gonna use.

It is quite apparent that independent of actual behavior manifested, as noted elsewhere (see Spencer, 1983, 1990), adolescents (and their parents) share the same values as the broader society and focus on their importance when asked. The following exchanges are instructive.

Interviewer: What advice would you give to new students starting the program this Fall? Since you'll be in your second year; we're going to look to you for leadership. So what are some things that you would tell new students coming into the program? If we had an orientation tomorrow and asked you to speak and say some things to the new students, what would you say? What are some thing you would say to them?

Christopher: I would tell them to do they work. You know what I mean. Listen everything people, they telling you. You know what I'm saying? Cause if you don't, you know what I mean, you never know who you going to end up in the future. You know what I'm saying? You be on the street somewhere.

Angel (Male): Well I start off with whatever bad habits you had at Piney Ridge, throw them away, just throw them away and start changing, because you're going to have different types of experience now you start in the SOS Program. And you're going to have to do a whole lot of different things that you never done at Piney Ridge High School and you have to be more responsible. Well … when they're right in front of me … then I say [it] a whole lot better.

Katrina's comments poignantly demonstrate the PVEST components, which link reactive coping strategies with identity processes and life stage outcomes. Her analysis is unusually insightful for a special education student and suggests that irrespective of the "objective criteria" used for special education placement, baseline social cognitive skills are available and afford directionality for social problem solving efforts.

Katrina: I would tell them to focus, not to play around, you know, to get something out of this and just to do they best and try to succeed, cause life is not a game, you know. Life is not nothing to play with, it's real, you know, and you gonna want something, then you gonna have to work hard for what you want in life. Can't play around and think you gonna get something handed to you, cause nothing is gonna be handed to you.

Discussion

When reviewing the responses of the students to the questions posed, it is important to remember that each is a special needs student; each student's academic experience is guided by an individual educational plan (IEP) as required by IDEA and Public Law 94–142. However, as noted by the various responses, all are uncommonly clear about the impact of context on their own behavior and their ability to focus on academic achievement and personal growth. Their analyses of the school setting at Piney Ridge, from a teacher's lack of interest to the disruptiveness of fellow students' behavior and their own involvement are very insightful … especially for young people who have been designated as having special educational needs.

Of particular salience were comments concerning their often challenging and stressful home life situations which are, more than likely, not "uncommon" and are associated with living in chronically low resource families and neighborhoods. Equally important is their own perceived responsibility to take an active role in solving family problems or difficult situations, which involve family members more generally. More related,

the fact that young people are burdened with myriad direct and indirect experiences of victimization and bereavement is significant and should have important implications for the level of support and quality of assistance required.

More specific, significant and specific resources are required for schools on a daily basis as opposed to the current fad, which is to have significant numbers of bereavement counselors and other mental health supports to "descend" on a school when a media-identified school level "loss" is experienced. Clearly, at some schools and in particular communities, consequential support is needed virtually on a daily basis if the impact of significant loss is not to become a chronic stressor which competes with academic requirements and long-term school achievement. There are educational and community settings which clearly require "extra supports" as an extension of traditional support staff.

The most striking "thematic" focus of all remarks across students had to do with the importance of having "caring" teachers. More often than not, the assumption of teachers when discussing student performance is that youth do not care about the educational process. However, when listening to youths' own voices, a critical motivator or barrier for on-task behavior is students' assumptions about whether or not teachers care (see Delpit 1995; Swanson et al., 1998). This view is inconsistent with many adult behaviors (both teachers and parents) based on assumptions about students' lack of concern and commitment. Too *infrequently* considered is that students may be "imitating" the same adult models who assume a lack of interest and commitment on the part of adolescents. That is why the use of a conceptual framework, which focuses on individuals' *own perceptions* and experiences is important for interpreting behavior. On the one hand, teachers may be under-performing, because they believe a lack of interest and concern on the part of adolescents. In response, adolescents may be deploying maladaptive (i.e., ego self-protecting) behaviors when they infer a lack of care and low expectations from teachers. The resulting dynamic is confusing, problematic, and produces assumptions of hopelessness on both sides. However, when considering deployed coping for both "individuals," (i.e. teacher and student), in terms of the PVEST framework, it would appear that each serves as a source of risk for the self and the other. That is, teachers in schools which are under-resourced, over-crowded, and with chronically difficult circumstances (e.g., significant episodic violence and loss) may have quite vulnerable professional egos. This "fragility" makes them less tolerant of transgressions (both real and assumed) and certainly less willing to "extend" themselves in understanding the perspective of others … "children" or not. On the other hand, students are under the same sources of psychological risk and fragility as their teachers; they, too, experience multiple-sourced stress, little buffering support, and are unable (and understandably unwilling) to take the perspective of the teachers. The point is made clearly by Rashae who describes his teacher's classroom behavior which, in fact, turns off his motivation and interest since it takes the teacher too long (i.e., after stopping to help other students) to get to him and provide help. He noted, "… she has to stop, talk to that student and stop and talk to that one and by then, you be like, never mind. So you just get tired of 'the hollering out her name.'" It is unmistakable that students and teachers engage in behavior at "cross-purposes" without actually being aware of the other's efforts. Each serves as a context of risk and stress for the other; neither is aware nor understands that each serves as the hope and the opportunity for the other's ego needs being met. That is, opportunities for professional success and sense of efficacy are not garnered by teachers, on the one hand; and skill acquisition and feelings of being respected, valued and cared for are likewise not experienced, on the other hand, by students.

It is this shared understanding by students, teachers, job coaches and work-site mentors that represents the context and underlying design for the structured and supported adult–student relationship of the Start-On-Success (SOS) program. This "shared understanding" is especially significant at particularly vulnerable periods of the life course. Bowlby (1982) describes the critically important "goal-corrected partnership" shared between parent and toddler which aids the child's safe passage through that vulnerable period between the second or third years of life (i.e., variously referred to as the "terrible twos"). The partnership also aids the quality of mental health for the assisting and guiding parent. Too few similar models of assisting and caring support are provided for adolescents who continue to be viewed with trepidation and fear. This is particularly the case when considering the social and schooling experiences of African American males (see Cunningham, 1993; 1994, 1999; Spencer, 1999; Spencer & Cunningham, in press).The objective stage of the life course called adolescence is a chronic stressor in and of itself. Adolescence is the point in the life course where youngsters are least often touched and for which the most negative and "normative" development-associated negative imagery and global trepidation is attached (i.e., "turbulent teen years," "terrible teens," etc.). Under the most supportive of conditions such monikers are stress exacerbating. For teens already burdened with negative imagery associated with their special needs category, investing in negative social and academic behavioral responses, although clearly *maladaptive coping* strategies from a PVEST framework, may serve short-term mental health needs. That is, the turning *away* from the very context (i.e., school

and learning opportunities) that provides a conduit for future successes may be a salve for mental health albeit in the *short run*. However, in the long run the coping behavior deployed, emergent identity evolved and virtually guaranteed outcomes only further exacerbate an already challenging set of circumstances and long term "expectations" associated with special needs categorization. That is, long term outcomes are sure to be even more difficult and less viable than the statistics currently predict. The qualitative data presented suggest that the Start-On-Success scholars program provides opportunities for more viable coping responses and adolescent growth-stimul*ating* insights, which guide behavior and provide supports for others. More specifically, Katrina makes the case quite eloquently when she notes what her own suggestions would be for a new student coming into the SOS program given her own experiences. She notes her counseling insights: "Life is not nothing to play with, it's real, you know, and you gonna want something, then you gonna have to work hard for *what* you want in life. Can't play around and think you gonna get something handed to you, cause nothing is gonna be handed to you." As suggested by the qualitative data reported, it is clear that the Start-On-Success Program provides a conceptual framework which successfully breaks down the negativity and (negative) stressful relationship between students and teachers. Teachers and students receive training and support, which emphasize that each is not permitted to serve as the "stimulus condition" for the other. Students have "transferable" skills, caring perspectives and penetrating insights which afford analyses that should bode well for long-term success.

References

Connell, J. P., Spencer, M. B., & Aber, J. L. (1994). Education risk and resilience in African-American youth: Context, self, action and outcomes in school. *Child Development, 65,* 493–506.

Cunningham, M. (1993). African American adolescent males sex role development. *Journal of African American Males Studies,* 1(1), 30–37.

Cunningham, M. (1994). *Expressions of manhood: Predictors of educational achievement of African American adolescent males.* Unpublished doctoral dissertation, Emory University, Atlanta, GA.

Delpit, L. (1995). *Other People's children: Cultural conflicts in the classroom.* New York: The New Press.

Duckenfield, M. & Swanson, L. (1992). Service learning: Meeting the needs of youth at-risk. A dropout prevention research report. Clemson, SC: National Dropout Prevention Center.

Erickson, E. H. (1968). *Identity: Youth and Crisis.* New York: Norton.

Fine, M. (1986). Why Urban Adolescents Drop Into and Out of Public High School. *Teachers College Record, 87* (Spring 1986), 393–409.

Gomez, J. J. (1989). The Path to School Based Management Isn't Smooth, But We're Scaling the Obstacles One by One. *The American School Board Journal* (October 1989), 20–22.

Graham, P. A. (1992). *S.O.S. Sustain Our Schools*. New York: Hill & Wang

Hamilton, S. F. (1986). Raising Standards and Reducing the Dropout Rate. *Teachers College Record, 87* (Spring 1986), 410–429.

Lechtenstein, G., McLaughlin, M., & Knudsen, J. (1991). *Teacher Empowerment and Professional Knowledge* (CPRE Research Report Series RR–020, 27, p. 1991). Stanford, CA: Stanford University, Center for Educational Policy Research.

McDill, E. L., Natriello, G. a. P., & Aaron, M. (1985). Raising standards and retaining students: The impact of the reform recommendations on potential dropouts. *Review of Educational Research, 55*(4), 415–433.

Nettles, S. M. (1991). Community contributions to school outcomes of African-American students. *Education and Urban Society, 24*(1), 132–147.

O'Connor, J. T. (1994). The Gift Denied, The Verse Unwritten. *Virginia Journal of Education*, (December, 1994).

Raywid, M. A. (1995). Making a difference for students at risk: Trends and alternatives. In M. C. Wang & M. C. Reynolds (Eds.), *Alternatives and Marginal Students*. Thousand Oaks, CA: Corwin Press.

Rodriguez, Garcia Y. (1997). Learned helplessness or expectancy-value? A psychological model for describing the experiences of different categories of unemployed people. *Journal of Adolescence, 20*, 321–333.

Spencer, M. B. (1983). Children's cultural values and parental child rearing strategies. *Developmental Review, 3*, 351–370.

Spencer, M. B. (1990). Parental values transmission: Implications for Black child development. In J.B. Stewart & H. Cheatham (Eds.), *Interdisciplinary perspectives on Black families* (pp. 111–130). New Brunswick, NJ: Transactions.

Spencer, M. B. (1995). Old Issues and New Theorizing about African American youth: A Phenomenological Variant of Ecological Systems Theory. In R.L. Taylor (Ed.), *Black Youth: Perspectives on Their Status in the United States* (pp. 37–69). Westport, CT: Praeger.

Spencer, M. B. (1999). Social and cultural influences on school adjustment: The application of an identity-focused ecological perspective. *Educational Psychologist, 34*(1), 43–57.

Spencer, M. B., Dupree, D., & Hartman, T. (1997). A Phenomenological Variant of Ecological Systems Theory (PVEST): A self-organization perspective in context. *Development and Psychopathology, 9*, 817–833.

Steinberg, L. D. (1988). Reciprocal relation between parent-child distance and pubertal maturation. *Developmental Psychology, 24*(1), 122–128.

Swanson, D. P., Spencer M. B., & Petersen, A. (1998). Identity Formation in Adolescence. In K. Borman & B. Schneider (Eds.), *The adolescent years: Social influences and educational challenges: Part 1. Ninety-seventh Yearbook of the National Society for the Study of Education*(pp. 18–41). Chicago: University of Chicago Press.

Wang, M.C., Haertel, G.D., & Walberg, H.J. (1997). *Fostering educational resilience in inner-city schools*. (LSS Publication Series, No. 4). Philadelphia: Temple University Center for Research in Human Development and Education.

Woolfolk, A. E. (1998). *Readings in Educational psychology*. 2nd Ed.

Received April 23, 1999
Final revision accepted August 15, 2000
Accepted December 12, 2000

INSTRUCTIONS FOR CONTRIBUTORS

Editorial Scope: The focus of *Applied Developmental Science* (*ADS*) is the synthesis of research and application to promote positive development across the life span. Applied developmental scientists use descriptive and explanatory knowledge about human development to provide preventive and/or enhancing interventions. The conceptual base of *ADS* reflects the view that individual and family functioning is a combined and interactive product of biology and the physical and social environments that continuously evolve and change over time. *ADS* emphasizes the nature of reciprocal person–environment interactions among people and across settings. Within a multidisciplinary approach, *ADS* stresses the variation of individual development across the life span—including both individual differences and within-person change—and the wide range of familial, societal, cultural, physical, ecological, and historical settings of human development.

The applied developmental science orientation is defined by three conjoint emphases. The *applied* aspect reflects its direct implication for what individuals, families, practitioners, and policymakers do. The *developmental* aspect emphasizes a focus on systematic and successive changes within human systems that occur across the lifespan. This assumption stresses the importance of understanding normative and atypical processes as they emerge within different developmental periods and across diverse physical and cultural settings. The *science* aspect stresses the need to utilize a range of research methods to collect reliable and objective information in a systematic manner to test the validity of theory and application.

The convergence of these three aspects leads to a fostering of a reciprocal relationship between theory and application as a cornerstone of applied developmental science, one wherein empirically based theory not only guides intervention strategies and social policy, but is influenced by the outcome of these community activities. Furthermore, it calls for a multidisciplinary perspective aimed at integrating information and skills drawn from relevant biological, social, and behavioral science disciplines.

Given this multidisciplinary orientation, *ADS* will publish research employing any of a diverse array of methodologies—multivariate-longitudinal studies, demographic analyses, evaluation research, intensive measurement studies, ethnographic analyses, laboratory experiments, analyses of policy and/or policy engagement studies, or animal comparative studies—when they have important implications for the application of developmental science across the life span. Manuscripts pertinent to the diversity of development throughout the life span—cross-national and cross-cultural studies; systematic studies of psychopathology; and studies pertinent to gender, ethnic, and racial diversity—are particularly welcome.

Audience: Developmental, clinical, school, counseling, aging, educational, and community psychologists; life course, family, and demographic sociologists; health professionals; family and consumer scientists; human evolution and ecological biologists; practitioners in child and youth governmental and nongovernmental organizations.

Manuscript Submission: Submit five manuscript copies (including five sets of illustrations, one of which is the original) and one disk copy (in both WordPerfect 5.1 and ASCII formats) to Dr. Richard M. Lerner, Editor, *Applied Developmental Science,* Center for Applied Child Development, Tufts University, 177 College Avenue, Medford, MA 02155 (E-mail: adsjournal@tufts.edu). All copies should be clear, readable, and on 8½ × 11-in. paper of good quality. Print text using 10-point (12-pitch) Courier or any other typeface that results in 1,800 to 2,000 characters per page (70 to 75 characters and spaces per line × 25 to 27 lines per page).

Prepare manuscripts according to the *Publication Manual of the American Psychological Association* (4th ed.). Any manuscript not in this style will automatically be returned to the author. Type all components of the manuscript double-spaced, including title page, abstract, text, quotes, acknowledgments, references, appendices, tables, figure captions, and footnotes. The abstract should be 100 to 150 words, typed on a separate sheet of paper. Authors must use nonsexist language in their articles. For information on this requirement, read "Guidelines for Nonsexist Language in APA Journals," which appeared in the June 1977 issue of *American Psychologist,* or consult the *APA Manual.* All manuscripts submitted will be acknowledged promptly. Authors should keep copies of their manuscripts to guard against loss. All manuscripts are reviewed by consultants with special competence in the area represented by the manuscript.

Tables: Refer to the *APA Manual* for format. Double-space. Provide each table with explanatory title; make title intelligible without reference to text. Provide appropriate heading for each column in table. Indicate clearly any units of measurement used in table. If table is reprinted or adapted from another source, include credit line. Consecutively number all tables.

Figures and Figure Captions: Figures should be (a) high-resolution illustrations or (b) glossy, high-contrast black-and-white photographs. Do not clip, staple, or write on back of figures; instead, write article title, figure number, and *TOP* (of figure) on label and apply label to back of each figure. Consecutively number figures. Attach photocopies of all figures to manuscript. Consecutively number captions with Arabic numerals corresponding to the figure numbers; make captions intelligible without reference to text; if figure is reprinted or adapted from another source, include credit line.

Articles and reviews must be judged to be of substantial importance to the broad, multidisciplinary readership of *ADS* as well as meet a high level of scientific acceptability. Manuscripts should include descriptions of participant populations, ethical procedures, research methods, and intervention strategies adequate for critique and replication. If not already described in the manuscript, a document describing the content and psychometric properties of any instruments used in the research that are not well-established in the literature is to be included with the manuscript at the time of submission.

Authors are responsible for all statements made in their work and for obtaining permission from copyright owners to reprint or adapt a table or figure or to reprint a quotation of 500 words or more. Authors should write to the original author(s) and publisher to request nonexclusive world rights in all languages to use the material in the article and in future editions. Provide copies of all permissions and credit lines obtained.

Only original manuscripts written in English are considered. In a cover letter, authors should state that the findings reported in the manuscript have not been published previously and that the manuscript is not being simultaneously submitted elsewhere. Authors should also state that they have complied with the ethical standards most relevant to their research discipline (e.g., guidelines from the American Psychological Association, the American Sociological Association, or the American Academy of Child Psychiatry). Upon acceptance, authors are required to sign a publication agreement transferring the copyright from the author to the publisher. Accepted manuscripts become the permanent property of the journal.

Production Notes: Authors' files are copyedited and typeset into page proofs. Authors read proofs to correct errors and answer editors' queries.